Life Compass Living™

A guide for growing up and growing old together

**BY GEORGE H. FULLER JR.,
D.MIN., M.DIV., MEDIATOR, CSA**

WITH APRIL KOONTZ, MSW

FORWARD BY AMY D'APRIX, MSW, PHD, CPCA

N|T NEWTYPE

Life Compass Living: A Guide for Growing Up and Growing Old Together

Cover Design by Adrial Designs
Interior Design by NEWTYPE Publishing
Interior Graphics by Adrial Designs
Story Editing by April Koontz
Text Editing by Melody Wilson

N|T NEWTYPE

Published by NEWTYPE Publishing
www.newtypepublishing.com
Paperback ISBN: 9781952421099
eISBN: 9781952421136

Library of Congress Control Number: 2020918588

First Edition
Printed in the United States.

This is for Elgin, Wake, Khora, Beckon, Haven,
and River (our grandchildren), as well as the
others coming along in our Family of Choice:
Kaleb, Addison, Raven, Cam, Hobbs, Ella, Noah,
Liam N, Natalie, Owen, Rowan, and Cooper,
and Isabella, Colton, Cora, Luke, and Liam T.

May we flourish together for your sakes!

Contents

Acknowledgments

The most important person in the story of Life Compass Living is my wife, Tammy. Her investment in this project is huge and it is mostly about how she loves me, our family, children, and learning. Much of any wisdom found in this book came from watching her love us and how she invited me to grow up and grow old with her.

There are many people who have encouraged me and invested time, money, and their very lives as Life Compass Living has taken shape since 2013. These people were essential in moments that made all the difference, and many continue to shape Life Compass Living and my Life Compass Plan. I wanted to attempt to collect the names so I could experience the buoyancy and express the gratitude they inspire. This is more a chronological list than their current place in how Life Compass Living is taking shape. My life and Life Compass Living needed the gifts they each gave: Hiram, Jay, Jake, Attsy, Gary, Dick, Ro, Penni, Jack P, Mary, Warren, Robert, Mary Ellen, Viola, Karolynn, RL, Tripp, Steven, Alecia, Chase, Steve C, Tricia C, Julius, Lula, Jacob, Luke C, Renee, Sue, Dana, Greg, Doug C, Danielle, Frank G, Kevin, Sue Ann, Matthew, Michelle, Bryson, Daniel, Ashley, Jamie, Dan, Christy, Leslie, Mike H, Andy, Ed, Beth, Roger N, Amy, Brian Mc, Philip, Phyliss, Steve S, David W, Jim, April, Neil,

Paula F, Aline, Kathy, Debbie, Linda L, Bob L, Roger Mc, Terri, Eric R, Cliff, Agnus, David M, Fred, Fairy, Alan S, Guy, Elaine, Jo Ann, Ken, Glenna, Ivan, Paula M, Alan M, Gay, Sophia, Eileen, Andrea, Beth, Neela, Mardi, Robin GW, Mike, Jasmine, John H, Al, Aidil, Doug, Nichole, Robin C, Scott, Perlie, Larry, Linda J, John R, Valerie, John P, Taylor, Jane, Victor, Luke B, Lyndsay, Vicki, Chris W, Zach, Amy, Scott P, Michelle, JT, Bob C, Anne, Nathan, Miriam, John C, Ashley, Jeffery, Eric S, Melody, Tricia G, Jennifer, Jack F, Nancy, Andrea, Tasha, Carolynn, Sara, Ron D, Denise, Ron W, Nelle, Terry, Kellan, Deborah, Chris H, Elizabeth, Miles, and my awesome Kickstarter Backers!

Making this list has led to tears of gratitude and confidence it is too short. I hope, as others cross my path and my mind, I will remember and say "thank you." I did not list the kind baristas in my coffee shops who welcomed me and cheered me on. OK, Stephanie has to get a shout-out!

The whole of my life exists in the Love that includes us all and will not let us go. I have come to know that Love in Jesus Christ. I hope I am faithful to all who have and continue to help me secure my soul (entire person), expand my mind, and keep walking into the horizon of **compassion and justice for everyone and everything**.

Foreword

When I graduated from college over 35 years ago with a degree in social work, I knew I wanted to help older people. What I didn't yet know, at that tender age, was that working with older people also meant working with their families. And that families come in all different shapes and sizes. I hadn't yet discovered that our lives look a lot like a beautiful spider's web, intricately connected with those closest to us. And, of course, I didn't yet have enough life experience to know that there are many common transitions that people go through as they move through the cycle of life.

My 35 years of working with, or on behalf of, older adults, their families, and the professionals who serve them have taught me some very important things. First and foremost, I've discovered that very few of us consciously prepare for the many life transitions that are part of living. And if we do prepare, we often approach this planning as if we're on a solo journey, rather than acknowledging our connectedness with those most important to us. I've also learned that many people equate "planning" with "financial planning," making the assumption that having enough money ensures a smooth journey through life. The result of this thinking is that we sacrifice quality of life and peace of mind — both for ourselves and for those we love.

Perhaps you're wondering if it's even possible to plan for all of the transitions in our lives? My answer to that question is a resounding yes! And, I believe the Life Compass Living protocol shows us the way. Discovering and living into the best version of ourself (Person), intentionally investing time, energy, and finances into our relationships (People), and getting clear on where "home"' is for each one of us (Place), can absolutely equip us for both the very common changes that occur in life *and* the "Life Quakes" (as George calls them) that erupt without notice.

I've known and worked with George for many years, and our philosophies are totally in sync. We're passionate about inspiring people to make plans that will allow more choice, control, and independence as they age and to truly maximize their quality of life. I couldn't be prouder to have my Essential Conversations framework included as an intricate part of the Life Compass discovery and planning process. In my mind, there's nothing more important than talking to our most important people about the most important things in our lives.

As you read this book, my hope is that the combination of our techniques will accomplish two things for you. The first is that your relationships with those involved in your life journey will be protected and significantly deepened. The second is that you'll move through life's transitions with more joy and fewer regrets.

No matter who you are; no matter your age; your life stage; your income level or profession, I'm confident Life Compass Living will enhance your future and the future of those who surround you.

Amy D'Aprix, MSW, PHD, CPCA
Toronto, Canada

Preface

"Mrs. Fuller, we have all the reports back from your CAT scan and biopsies. What we are dealing with is Stage Four Non-Hodgkin's lymphoma."

It's an early-morning doctor's visit in February 2001, and these are *not* the words I want to hear travel from an oncologist's mouth to my mom's ears.

It is good I was recording the conversation, because the ensuing shock faded out key parts of my memory. I felt foolish when I went back later and listened to some of the questions I asked:

"How many stages are there?" I asked.

"Four," he replied.

"Do they start with 'four' and count down, or start with 'one' and count up?"

"There are four stages. 'Four' is the last stage. This means that the cancer has metastasized to several locations. The cancer is in the liver, spleen, several lymph nodes, and … well, I know this is a lot to take in, but we have treatment options."

Mom: "So, this is the end?"

Doctor: "Mrs. Fuller, we can extend your life and give you some good days. This cancer responds well to some particular chemotherapy, but at this stage we are not able to prevent a recurrence. I believe you will qualify for a research project that shows some hope of long-term remission."

Mom, "That's it. I don't want any treatment. It's the Lord's will, and I'm ready."

In that moment, I took on a role I would have for 13 years: I was now on a "care team."

A care team is a support group sharing the journey with people fighting to live well while battling sickness, disability, or death. Any of these can occur without notice or as part of the "normal" process of aging. This news began a steady and continuous series of health challenges in our family. The challenges included my wife, Tammy, who had advanced cancer. My dad had Alzheimer's, advanced lung cancer and other less ominous conditions. My mother-in-law had the long progression of MRSA. My father-in-law faced off with congestive heart failure, diabetes, high blood pressure and other issues that go along with aging.

Back in the exam room, I asked my mom to listen to all the options before we made decisions. She agreed. The rest of the appointment took 53 minutes. She understood that the clinical trial she qualified for would be a very difficult treatment protocol that included heavy chemotherapy and a bone marrow transplant. She agreed to "give a try" for reasons that were consistent with who my mom was.

She said, "If you can learn things that will help others beat this thing, then I want to help you learn what you need to learn. Hiram (that's my dad), I'm sorry you have to go through this, but if you are OK with it, then I'll do what we need to do."

My dad nodded at me and said, "George, we can do this."

I said, "Of course we can. Fullers don't give up without a fight."

It was a two-year fight. She died on February 13, 2003; this extra time allowed Mom to be present for the wedding of my oldest son, my youngest son's high school graduation and a host of other joy-filled moments.

This is what started my journey of intentional living, growing, and facing head-on the aging process and ultimate reality that we as human beings will one day die. Perhaps, it's more accurate to say it is how my journey "expanded." We are always on that journey and, *sometimes*, we notice.

I didn't know how to navigate these challenges well. I *hated* not knowing how to help those I love, including myself, have a good life.

The experiences of those 13 years included a mandate that resulted in this book. I see now that much of what drove me to learn and plan was for my own protection, and a way for me to maintain some amount of control. Unfortunately, I didn't have the foresight to see the full impact my decisions would eventually have on my entire family. For example, the college debt we're still paying off today because of money that was moved from the future of my boys to the care of those in crisis. I can't help but think that our parents would have wanted us to save more for the young people they loved so much. We all took time off of work without a discussion of who could afford it and how our financial resources would be replenished. Now I realize that we could have minimized the impact on our financial plans for both the short and long term if we had simply paused and talked openly as a family. In retrospect, I see so many places we could have saved money, honored boundaries, made memories, and involved a wider circle of people for strength and support.

As we went through those years of caregiving, we were doing the best we could to live our own lives — adding spouses, babies, friends, and moving in and out of jobs. Fortunately, I had the gift of time with a counselor and a spiritual director who helped me navigate the personal struggles that emerged during this time. I spent hours in what I call my "chair," struggling to face my weaknesses, embrace my strengths, and ultimately make the decision of who I wanted to be and how I wanted to live. I dove into research about the various health conditions that had impacted the ones I love, the process of aging, and the complex world of products, professionals, programs, and services that often felt like an avalanche chasing me down a mountain. Many days, my biggest challenge was following my dad's encouragement to "keep your pecker up." (That was his crude way of describing the ability to maintain a sense of joy in the small space between laughter and tears that we call "real life.") I know some of you will face everything that I went through without the supportive family, "enough" money, and good friends I had. This book is for all of us, but especially you.

So, let's dive into *you*.

When was the last time you thought about "growing" into the rest of your life, more aware and more intentionally?

Who will you "be" to the babies being born into your life now and in the future? What role will you play in their individual lives as they begin their journeys? If you're their parent, have you thought about the legacy you want to leave them? Have you considered what you want them to know about living and dying and when you want them to know it? Have you thought about what impact your aging process will have on them and how to protect them from undue emotional, physical, financial, and even spiritual stress? If you're their relative or family friend, will you be an active participant in their lives and develop a personal relationship with them, despite a significant geographical distance, or will you be more of an acquaintance who keeps up with them from afar?

Which of your friends do you want to share the "whole of life" with? Meaning, who will you jump into life's mud with, no matter what sacrifices it will require on your part? Do they know it? Do you know which friends will be there with and for you when you're in the mud?

Is your career facilitating your ability to maintain the life and relationships you want? Are you working in a job that gives you life or sucks the life out of you?

Will the life you are living now provide for you and those you love while creating a legacy worthy of your life?

Is finishing life well something you consciously plan for, or is contemplating "the end" an overwhelming mass of details and dread that you tend to block out?

If you don't have answers and plans for these questions, I understand. I didn't, either. And I'm still continuously working on them. This book will not give you the answers that are particular to the life you share with your people, but I believe you'll find what you need to guide the Essential Conversations you need to have in your own soul and with the people you love most. You will also have a process that will empower you to make life plans so you can enrich your relationships and secure your future. As we begin, we will look at the challenges and then we will address them in ways that fit real life as well as our own hopes, potential, and limitations.

WHERE WE'RE GOING

Lao Tzu said, "The journey of a thousand miles begins with a single step." — I would like to add, "Maps don't get you there, but they can show you the way."

I wrote this book with the hope that the images, language, and concepts would be accessible to anyone who enters adolescence and the adventure of self-knowledge and self-determination while understanding that life is directed mostly by the adults. If you want to explore the complexity and science, check out the works in the bibliography and have fun. I spent five years sorting through the huge treasure of insights and wisdom that informs the Life Compass Living community.

The map that shows the way to Life Compass Living is a protocol. My wife, Tammy, is an educator, and she often reminds me that conversations, meetings, and decision-making go much better when we have a protocol. Here's the definition she gave me that guides her work in school reform and now our own "family meetings."

> *"Protocols are structured processes and guidelines to promote meaningful, efficient communication, problem-solving, and learning. Protocols give time for active listening and reflection, and ensure that all voices in the group are heard and honored. Using protocols appropriately in meetings with others helps you build the skills and culture necessary for productive collaborative work."*

The Life Compass Plan Protocol is what we will learn in this book. As we begin to have what we call our Essential Conversations (talking to the most important people about the most important things in our lives) guided by each person's Life Compass (Person, People, Place) we will be able to accomplish the mission of the Life Compass Living community:

> *"We help one another flourish in every stage of life, and manage life transitions with elegance. We do that by helping one another create LIFE COMPASS PLANS to build the lives we want, with the People we want, in the Place we want. We help one another put those Plans together and find the resources to make them a reality."*

Welcome to Life Compass Living! Let's get started!

CHAPTER 1

Mapping Your Life's Journey Using The Life Compass Plan

"If one advances confidently in the direction of his dreams, and endeavors to live the life which he has imagined, he will meet with a success unexpected in common hours." — Henry David Thoreau

THE CHALLENGE WE FACE TOGETHER

We exist at a critical point in history and, as a result, share a conundrum. The ways we were taught to grow up and grow old were created in a world that no longer exists, and we're suffering. The awesome technology that allows us to be across our continent in four hours and around the world within a day has also stolen our "aging heritage." We're suffering from anxiety, depression, and a multitude of physical ailments directly related to stress. Many of us are lonely despite the hundreds and thousands of "friends" across our social media accounts and the number of Likes, Shares, and Retweets on our posts. We have trouble sleeping and staying healthy, and we long to feel better. Our children are feeling pressure in a way that we couldn't imagine at their age. The days and events of our lives seem to pass by us at the speed of a rocket. We're living longer, the makeup of families and communities is shifting, jobs are elusive, "retirement" is being radically reinvented, and, on top of it all, the programs, products, and services that we need and depend on throughout our lives have become very complex and expensive. Modern life has become so segmented that we find ourselves unable to create a mutuality — a "we" space — that secures our babies, our young adults, our middle-aged adults, and our older adults all inside wise and compassionate plans.

I found the transitions of adult life challenging. From high school graduation to my current life as a business owner and grandparent (I go by "Gpops"), my wife, Tammy, and I have been diligent partners. We raised our kids to the best of our abilities and, like most, the extent of our "life planning" included the hopes to finance our kids' college tuition and our retirement. Being prepared for the needs of our aging parents or one of us having cancer was never in the picture. As our parents headed toward the end of their lives and their needs increased, we did the best we could with the knowledge we had, but I felt intimidated and inadequate. There were vital resources we needed to support them that we were unaware of until late in the process. I hated the cost of my ignorance. That is when I realized that, while I was taught many good things that shaped my life, I was not taught how to navigate through all of life's transitions — from the cradle to the grave and everything in between — with the people I love. I needed a plan or I would continue to be ill-prepared, waste resources, and even be toxic to myself and others.

This need led me to do some research and some deep soul exploration. I knew there had to be a way out of the quagmire of overwhelming angst and the feeling of "is this all there really is?" We're born. We grow up. We find partners. Some of us have kids. Some of us choose careers. We save a few bucks here and there to go on vacation. We throw birthday parties and weddings and dress up for Halloween. Then we get sick and die. Depressing? Yes. I was in a tough spot. The deaths of my parents and Tammy's parents, and then Tammy being sick was almost more than I could bear. My heart was broken. My religion inadequate. I knew I needed — and greatly suspected that others needed — a way to more consciously share life, connect to the needed resources, and fully leverage the strengths found in *each* life stage — not just the beginning and the end. It was through these dark days that the idea of Life Compass Living — Person, People, Place, Plan — was born.

As we begin to explore the idea of Life Compass Living, it's important to first understand what we're up against. I see four distinct challenges that must be faced in order to build our lives together, and they all begin with the letter C: *Current. Currency. Community Crisis. Constant Change.*

1. Current

Think about it. Since the second electricity lit up the night, we've been filling every hour with work, experiences, and interactions. We've become a world of constant stimulation and social engagement. We're "on" all the time, and it's creating an epidemic of loneliness and addictions, as well as significant damage to our health.[1] We move from one thing to the next at a breakneck pace. Our minds are chasing the alluring sources of feel-good fixes at our fingertips. What's getting lost in the process? Everyday *mindfulness.* We're missing precious moments of just "being," the crux of where the magic happens between our conscious and unconscious minds. The place where we ponder and explore what we value as individuals and experience the nudgings of the Divine. The space where spontaneous conversations happen and deeper understanding occurs. To live and create an intentional community, we have to be willing to create more time to unplug, more time to talk to each other, more time to sit with ourselves in the larger story — the larger reality that we're part of — and frame our lives with the principles and values that will hold us and our future generations solidly in place.

For most of human history, there was time to be together, to talk and be mindful. Why? Because there was this thing called *darkness*. There were seasons to work and seasons to rest. There were rituals that followed the way the Earth moved in relation to the sun that held us together in the cycles of day and night, the seasons of the year, and sacred times of renewal, remembrance, and community. There was a simplicity and rhythm to life. Then came electricity and the innovations of the industrial and digital age, and all of a sudden, life became more and more complicated. Now we can easily stay engaged every moment of a 24-hour day and escape the world of responsibilities with an almost limitless list of options. We are in the *current,* and it won't end unless we schedule time to unplug. From the second our alarm goes off, the *current* greets us. Our cellphones sit in anticipation on the nightstand, hungry to share every notification and alert from every app we've downloaded or contact we've added. With the rush of dopamine that comes from a swipe up or down, it's no wonder we've been captured, and many of us imprisoned, in the *current's* seductive trance. It's time for us to wake up to the collective "sleep" we're in at the global, national, and individual level. **Our kids are depending on us to make this change.** If it feels too overwhelming to go for a day without your phone, start with 15-30 minutes in the morning. If you use your phone as an alarm clock, turn the alarm off and put it down. Consider making your family dinners a "no phone zone" or playing the game at a restaurant that whoever looks at their phone first pays the bill. The next time you choose to jump on Facebook while sitting at a stoplight or finish your game of solitaire while standing in a checkout line, remember the hold the *current* has on you and decide whether it's worth succumbing to it. Think about what opportunities you might miss during those few moments. Perhaps someone near you is having a lonely day and would benefit from your smile or an insight to a question you've been carrying? Technology is an extraordinary gift, except for when it steals hours and days and years of our lives that we'll never get back. *Current* is a challenge we must face if we're going to do the work of discovering and building lives that hold rich meaning. Every second counts.

2. *Currency*

The next profound challenge builds on the first, and I call it *currency*. It causes us to lose touch with one another without even noticing. Here's how it works. For millennia, trade was exchanging things of value: your cow for my chicken; your wheat for my corn; my spice for your labor. It wasn't always fair, and there were abuses, but trade was literally trading. Eventually, some humans felt this process of trade could happen more quickly and efficiently if we replaced a literal object, like a cow or chicken or wheat or corn, with an abstract "stand-in" object that represented a particular amount of value. This *currency*, from Middle English: *curraunt*, "in circulation," was composed of precious metals at first, and then paper. Now, most *currency* is made up of electrons in digital bank transactions — little more than an idea. As trade became abstracted, so did relationships. So much so that we've become disconnected from our common humanity. We've become divorced from the Earth and less aware of the contributions and dependencies held in our "purchases." Consequently, our consumption is increasingly compulsive. We chase the products, experiences, and security that at one time existed only within our community. And the more we chase, the less we feel satisfied.

Recently, I had an insight about all of this trade, currency, value, and connection stuff that I found helpful. But before I share it, let me make a confession: I'm a person who loves coffee. If I'm honest, I've become — in spite of my best efforts — a bit of a coffee snob. Besides being somewhat particular when it comes to java, I also have three coffee shops that I frequent. I love seeing my People there, and I love my barista friends handing me a cup of coffee. It's a very "whole-person" experience for me. What I often miss is all that is held inside the *currency* that moves when I scan the barcode on the app or slow everyone down by pulling out cash. I end up buying that cup of joe as if it just appeared out of thin air. It's a fair trade, right? $3.33, including a tip, for something that just "happened" to appear?

In reality, if I would unplug from the *current* that keeps me continuously engaged, if I would become mindful of what this *currency* transaction actually represents, then I could, in that moment, realize that the Earth not only created the coffee plant, but that it brought the beans to maturity. Further, some person who has a family picked those beans, and another group of people — who also have families — brought those beans to a market. Some people who have families ran the market, collected the beans, and shipped them to a warehouse, and people with families ran that warehouse and took the beans to a roaster. People with families roasted those beans just the way I like them, and — yes — some people with families transported those roasted beans to my coffee shop, where some people with families took those beans, ground them, and brewed them just right, handing me my cup of coffee. When that $3.33 was transacted, I actually received the work of the Earth and many of her families, human and nonhuman alike.

This simple realization was what catalyzed me to buy Certified Fair Trade coffee. It costs a bit more but this simple practice allowed me to know that, when I transferred *currency*, it would be distributed more equitably to everyone — all the different parts — that brought this cup to me. I could give invisible partners the dignity of a living wage.

As a result of this simple act of awareness and action, drinking a cup of coffee has become much more than a morning ritual to me. It is a vehicle through which I connect to the soil and families that work those lands in varied cultures. I began to see that the person handing me the cup of coffee was actually sharing life with me — their life and the lives of countless others. Now, I've moved from having *my* cup of coffee to having *our* cup of coffee.

Economists more specialized than me will argue that we've gained much by using *currency*; our complex economy makes wealth more mobile than ever, creating livelihoods and commerce in the process. There is undoubtedly some truth to this, alongside some very real loss and difficulty for those struggling financially. But even in this rosiest of economic outlooks, can we acknowledge the very real loss we encounter on the level of felt-experience?

The notion of *currency* is something that creates an imagined separation between me, the consumer, and the people involved in producing the thing I'm "buying." I end up experiencing a profound disconnection from others by mindlessly transacting *currency* over and against the deep satisfaction of doing my part in supporting all of us.

Like *current, currency* is a challenge we must face as we choose to live a life based on our Life Compass. The next time you buy a cup of coffee or an ice cream cone or a shirt from a department store, remember the people who have been involved in the process of getting that "good" to you. This simple awareness is a foundational piece of creating a Shared Life together.

3. Community Crisis

Beyond *current* and *currency*, we're also experiencing a *community crisis*. I mentioned this earlier when I talked about the changes facing families and communities, but I want to revisit this more deeply here. Our families and our communities have been deconstructed. We have moved away, both literally and figuratively, and we have not yet reconstructed the sources of support they provided for us. Sometimes we left for good reasons. I want to encourage the search for a supportive environment when we find ourselves in a toxic one. Even when we left for good reasons, we often didn't land in communities with all the support systems in place that we needed. We didn't notice what we lost in the midst of finding some good things and good people.

I watched the movie "Cars" with my grandchildren. Actually, I watched it many times and realized that I connected with the characters in ways my grandchildren couldn't yet. This was particularly true every time the song "Our Town" would come on. It was written by Randy Newman and performed by James Taylor, who are part of my generation. I mostly laughed and cheered for Lightning McQueen. But these lyrics caused me to stop and grieve the loss of our towns, even though they were far from perfect.

"Long ago, but not so very long ago
The world was different, oh yes, it was
You settled down and you built a town and made it live
And you watched it grow, it was your town

"Time goes by, time brings changes, you changed too
Nothing comes that you can't handle, so on you go
You never see it coming when the world caves in on you
On your town, nothing you can do

"Main street isn't main street anymore
Lights don't shine as brightly as they shone before
To tell the truth, lights don't shine at all in our town
Sun comes up each morning, just like it's always done
Get up, go to work, start the day
You open up for business that's never gonna come
As the world rolls by a million miles away

Main street isn't main street anymore
"No one seems to need us like they did before
It's hard to find a reason left to stay
But it's our town, love it anyway
Come what may, it's our town"

Today many of us have a multitude of social connections that include a copious amount of shared experiences, from dinners out to adventurous trips, to you name it. And we have the selfies to prove it. But the loneliness people speak of in candid moments is generated by our lack of looking, and learning, and planning to build the deep mutuality and interdependence that we need to secure our lives now and in the future. We are also missing the multi-generational relationships that teach us how to truly care for and honor one another during each stage of life. We each have a family and a community we were born into. However, most of us share life with a Family of Choice that includes People we may not be related to, and we likely live a long way from where our lives began. This is an opportunity to flourish together wrapped in the challenges of building a Shared Life with our Family of Choice.

One of the questions I like to ask people — whether in my local neighborhood or in Life Compass Living workshops continent-wide — is: "Whose diapers will you change and who will change yours?" This question seems to literally stun people. Their eyes are like a deer in headlights. Pause for a moment and ask yourself that question. Isn't changing diapers what living in community is all about? Shared vulnerability. Knowing someone has your back, no matter what the situation? Isn't that the sacred part of giving and receiving love in the dirty, raw moments of our humanity? One thing that everyone seems hungry for is *connection*. People are hungering for deeper relationships. Oddly, even though we long to take this road less traveled, we often just gaze flatly at the map, feeling even more isolated. We long to be together in ways that enrich one another's lives, but when it comes to becoming intimate, to deeply understanding each other, we often simply avoid the work that has to be done to create those kinds of relationships. I believe wisdom around this *community crisis* is more a matter of survival than we realize. It's been said that we "… without ever quite intending to — have become the first humans to ever dismantle our tribes."[2] I know in my soul that we can reverse that trend.

4. Constant Change

The final challenge I want to highlight is the brutal truth of *constant change*. In a stable world of sameness, life would be hard enough. I don't think we can overestimate the impact of constantly being given options and realizing the ground we walk on is dissolving. We're having to make more decisions than ever, and there will be more decisions tomorrow. These decisions include who we connect with and where, how we eat, what we'll watch on the numerous screens, who we trust for our news and information, and so much more. At the deepest levels, we are becoming explorers looking for our identities and a Place to belong in a smorgasbord of spiritualities, social connections, and global crises.

So, it's not just about TV shows or podcasts; there are some huge decisions on the line:

- What religious tradition will we take part in, if any?
- What politics will we align with, if any?
- Who will we surround ourselves with?
- Where will we live?
- What is our vocation and how long will it endure?
- Where will we spend our time and money?

On and on it goes. We need to recommit to the hard work of mindfully sorting out our lives: Who we are, what we want, where we want to go, and who we want to go with. I believe we can do it, but we'll have to do it intentionally. It's challenging, and many of us will avoid it to our own detriment. Remember, the greatest joys and grandest victories are reserved for those who love well in the crucible of real life.

I can remember my father lamenting about how fast things were changing, and I thought it was a bit funny because I was young at the time, mindlessly enjoying all the comfort found in the privileged life given to me. Now, I'm older. I've turned 60 and, as I remember his words, I wish I could apologize for my attitude toward him because he was right. Change is overwhelming. It's a constant. Every day brings something new. When I try to find and follow wisdom in the midst of this *constant change*, I find it hard, and yet it *is* there and it's ours to find. Accidental fools still suffer together. We can't slow change down but we can deliberately surf its waves and avoid being hit by a tsunami.

In light of these challenges, I'd like to orient you on how to use this book. As you learn the Life Compass Plan, I want us to take a 10,000-foot view of how to put *your* Life Compass Plan together. First off, remember this is a process guided by a protocol. It is intended to promote meaningful, efficient communication, problem-solving, learning and decision-making. Protocols give time for active listening and reflection, and ensure that all voices in the group are heard and honored. I offer this invitation without judgment attached. I am encouraging us to talk and think together with the People in our lives so we can build unique plans for how we can grow and thrive emotionally, spiritually, physically, and financially together. Yes, we can do this together.

Remember, the greatest joys and grandest victories are reserved for those who love well in the crucible of real life. will discover in these pages.

THE LIFE COMPASS

As I briefly mentioned earlier in this chapter, Life Compass Living has four parts that make for human flourishing: Person, People, Place (Life Compass) and a Plan that makes it a reality. Simply said, to flourish, we need to discover and live into (and out of) the best version of ourselves as a *Person*. We need a group of *People* with whom we experience the shared intentionality and directionality of doing life together. And this needs to take place where our life stories and our contributions are truly valued and expressed. Our Plans will enrich the Person we are becoming, the People who are with us, and the shape of the Place where we live through every twist and turn on life's journey. We will describe each part in detail, but for now just know that we truly flourish when we plan to live the lives we truly want.

WHY A LIFE COMPASS?

A compass is an old tool for finding our way to where we want to go. I think it's a great metaphor for what we need to help us find and follow our "true north" as we navigate our journey. When I use the phrase "true north," I'm referring to staying true to our Person, People, and Place through our various life stages. If you were living where I live — in Raleigh, North Carolina — and decided to walk to the Pacific Ocean on the other side of the continent, you might want to have a map or a GPS that tells you how to get from Point A to Point B. These types of tools are a lot more specific than life often is. We don't always know exactly where we'll end up, exactly where we want to be, but we do have a direction in mind: We start to form values, goals, dreams, and a purpose — maybe several purposes — that guide our lives.

With a Life Plan guided by the elements of Person, People, and Place, we can get up each morning and reorient ourselves in the direction of our destination of choice. It empowers us to direct our lives toward what we have identified as meaningful and important without losing our way to the overwhelming distractions that bombard us daily. Since life is an ever-changing journey that we don't have complete control over, the Person, People, Place elements allow us to love the day we are living in and adjust our Plans together, regardless of what comes our way. For example, there will be People who come into our lives and walk with us the entire journey. There will also be People who stay with us for only a season. There may be a Place we live our entire lives. Or there may be different Places where we live. As long as we're focused on these three elements throughout our lives and stay current with the People important to us, we can plan to live in alignment with our values, which is the biggest contributor to our ability to weather life's storms. Life Compass Living is guided by the Life Compass at both an individual and community level. Through conversations and planning, life becomes a shared adventure.

ESSENTIAL CONVERSATIONS

One of my People is an incredibly insightful and gifted woman named Amy D'Aprix. "Dr. Amy," as she's often called, is an internationally renowned expert on life transitions related to caregiving, retirement, aging, and family dynamics. With a master's degree and Ph.D. in social work, a background in gerontology, and years of acting as the primary caregiver for a multitude of people, Dr. Amy has a wealth of both book and street smarts. As friends and colleagues, Amy and I share the same life passion: Helping folks have the conversations they need to have in order to move through life's transitions with more joy and fewer regrets. Once we discovered this shared passion, we decided to combine the material she's developed on Essential Conversations along with my material on Life Compass Living.

Life Compass Living is powered by **Essential Conversations**, which are all about **talking to the most important people about the most important things in our lives.** It's the fuel that brings life to our Life

Compass Plan. By using the Essential Conversations tools as your guide, your Life Compass will take shape and be reshaped as you mindfully and compassionately discover the Person you are becoming, those People you wish to share life with, and the Place where your lives will unfold in our world. Your conversations will take on deep and lasting meaning and enrich the way you relate to yourself and those you love. You'll discover how to welcome the People who come into your life later, and graciously let go of those who need to take a different path. The story of human history is moving in a direction that demonstrates the consequences of how we share our lives and our biosphere. We cannot escape the connectedness of everything and all of us. I like to say, "We are all related. The only choice we have is how we relate." We can do the work, and it will make all the difference!

LIFE COMPASS PLAN

A Life Compass Plan is made up of the practical steps we each take to follow our Life Compass, thus living life as we choose. It is also a Plan created by those who want to share life at some level. The degree of intimacy and interdependence, as well as the location and longevity of the relationships, will be determined by the nature of the relationships unfolding in real life. We will also connect with the resources we need to make our Plans reality. For Life Compass Living, a resource is anything or anyone that meets a current or future need in our Plan.

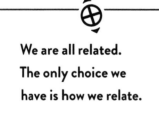

We are all related. The only choice we have is how we relate.

The magic of a Life Compass Plan is that everyone has one. As we create our individual Plans together, we will honor and support the Life Compass of each Person in our constellation, because we are each valuable and unique. Even my two sons, whom I love dearly, and whose lives I (and my wife) desire to be intimately part of, each have their own Life Compass. They have different People in *their* lives.

They're in different communities, and they each have different dreams. The places where their stories are unfolding and their contributions are being made are not the same places where my wife and I live. They may be one day, but in the meantime, our family fully honors and mutually supports each member's Life Compass.

Life Compass Living is also about honoring the Dignity of Choice, the reality that each person is unique, and the truth that we will all make our own set of mistakes, progress, and regressions. The allies and role models you will meet in the Life Compass Living community are not going to be ideal-life dreamers chasing goals in isolation. Instead, you'll join real-life planners helping one another reduce the vulnerabilities that are part of life and realize more of the possibilities held in our highest hopes.

I love imagining the beautiful diversity that will be created in the Life Compass Living community. Within our unique differences, we will find we have much in common. We will learn from one another and, in this learning, we will better understand the complexities of the human experience as well as those things that are available within and around us to help us securely navigate each life transition.

It starts with you, the Person who will take the time to read this book, to think through this rich set of concepts and action steps, and — with the People in your life — talk through what you will discover in these pages.

Life Compass Living is *transformational*. The kinds of changes that you'll be making will not only meet the needs of your current reality, but they will transform the relationships you have and the legacy you choose to create with your life.

The illustration below provides a visual tool of our Life Compass. We'll use the tool to quickly find our "true north" as we navigate life's often messy and tenuous terrain.

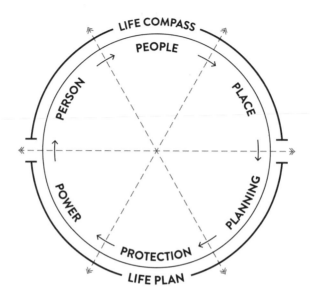

Moving through the process will be a continuous progression beginning with Person but you can actually start anywhere in the process that moves around the circle based on a current need or crisis. I have had many clients start with Protection in a crisis and others who had to find some Provisions for a current need before giving their Life Compass full attention. It is our hope that the work of knowing and sharing your Life Compass will inform and shape a Life Plan, thus making it a Life Compass Plan. Our "true north" includes all of the elements. As we practice using our Life Compass, we'll become better at discovering and intentionally planning to live as our best selves (Person), with those we love (People), and to be at home along the way (Place).

By honoring our own Life Compass and those of others, we're better able to manage our expectations and determine how to best respond to the people and situations life presents us.

For example, I know a person who is one of those mindful souls who seems to be able to be present and content no matter what is happening.

He moves in harmony with his Life Compass, which doesn't always include much of a Plan. We've talked about the lessons we've learned trying to be religious, professional, compassionate, and responsible as we love the People in our lives. He has moved through several professions with less focus on what guarantees him a retirement plan and the wealth some of us wish for him. We believe he's vulnerable because of his lack of planning and his unwillingness to stay put in the roles our culture rewards with financial and relational security. I'll have to admit that we also envy him in many ways. He has a contentment with who he is and seems to be at home in whatever situation faces him. I've had conversations with his life partner (a compassionate adventurous soul) who likes to plan for their financial future. She has learned to make important decisions for herself while continuing to live in a relationship with him. These decisions haven't been easy. However, the plans she's made have allowed them to remain in the relationship they treasure while honoring their individual Life Compasses with less fear and resentment. It is beautiful to watch.

You may have People in your life who will choose to follow a Life Compass without a Plan. We need to honor those People and their choices without attempting to put them in the shackles of a Life Plan they haven't chosen. However, we also need to determine how and to what extent we will support them when they go through a life transition crisis. These transitions are not an "if," they are a "when." Aging is hard. As we lose our independence,

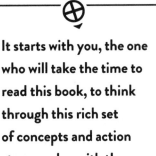

It starts with you, the one who will take the time to read this book, to think through this rich set of concepts and action steps, and — with the people in your life — talk through what you will discover in these pages.

our needs increase. Watching someone you love go through the aging process, or face a Life Quake (a Life Transition that happens without notice or without a plan) without the resources to accommodate their increased needs can lead to our own emotional, spiritual, and even financial bankruptcy. There are Essential Conversations that need to occur and sometimes difficult decisions that need to be made with respect to the vulnerabilities that come with choosing to live a Life Compass without a Plan.

A common choice in our consumer society is living with a Plan solely focused on finances. This is the opposite scenario of the above example. When our Life Compass is reduced to securing a life partner, finding a job, and making a financial plan, we often forfeit the richness of our Core Relationships. I worked with a client who has the most complete Plan I've ever seen in terms of providing financial security for his family and getting things done that he commits to do. He would be the envy of most of the people I know. I learned a great deal from him about being organized, responsible, completing tasks, and providing for the financial security of a family. He did not need anyone to teach him any of those skills. He was qualified as a role model of planning. When we sat together, the challenges he faced were in his relationships and how he could shape the legacy he would leave in his work and family. His family wasn't aware of all he had done — and was continuing to do — to financially secure their lives. His absence during his working years and his focus on sticking to the plan he had formed (with them in mind), left the family disconnected emotionally. His wife and kids were both grateful and resentful because of his lack of presence. More than his money, they wanted *him*. They wanted to know him as a Person — his likes and dislikes, his dreams and fears. And they wanted him to know the same of them. They wanted to share life experiences *with* not without him. I was encouraged to see the lightbulbs in their minds and hearts turn on when they realized it wasn't an "either/or" scenario but rather "both/and." This insight is the stepping stone into Life Compass Living together and the beginning of enriching their way of sharing life.

It's amazing to experience the power of honest communication. It is through our Essential Conversations that we discover and blend each person's Life Compass into a Shared Life Vision, thus creating a Life Compass Plan. As we begin to look at each part of the Life Compass, please fight the temptation to seek perfection or complete security and safety from the nature of real life. It won't shield us from joy or pain. It's meant simply to be a guide to discover the life you want and then direct your choices toward realizing that life. It will still be risky, but with this clarity you will be less vulnerable and free to be more adventurous.

WHAT DOES IT MEAN TO FLOURISH?

In case you haven't noticed, I mention the word flourish a lot. In my mind, it's a word that encompasses all we're working toward in Life Compass Living. Like every word in any language, it holds energy and even power. When we speak or even *think* words, we're putting energy into the world. So, what we say or think about ourselves and others can truly impact our mental and physical health. If you haven't read about the power of words, I suggest you look into it. You'll truly be amazed. Anyway, what I'm getting ready to say here is very powerful and holds forward-moving energy. Ready? "It is time for us to claim our right to flourish!" Say that again. Slowly.

If you're like my friends and family, you're probably thinking to yourself, "Uh, OK, George. Yeah. Let's all claim our right to flourish, whatever that means." I'll concede that this is a

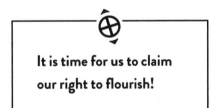

It is time for us to claim our right to flourish!

bit of a "head in the clouds" statement. A topic as broad as *human flourishing* is bound to be complex, but I want to unpack this in a way we can all understand.

When I say we're engaging in a journey toward what it means to *fully flourish*, I simply mean we're choosing to discover what it means for us, as individuals, to plan to live our lives to the fullest — individually (Person), in relationship with others (People), and in our community at large (Place). Before we explore the first area — Person — let's drill down to what I've found in my research to be four basic and core elements of human flourishing:

1. Mindfulness
2. Core Relationships
3. Physical Vitality
4. Mental Vitality

Mindfulness

First, there's mindfulness. Mindfulness is the basic human ability to be fully present, aware of where we are and what we're doing, and not be overly reactive or overwhelmed by what's going on in us and around us. Mindfulness helps us to be with ourselves, to be with the stories we tell ourselves in our mind, and to observe ourselves as part of a larger story with less anxiety and the need to be in control. This equips us to exercise the responsibility of self-determination (how I live my life) and self-actualization (living my life to its fullest potential) from a place of peace and openness. It's also the place, in my experience, where we come to understand that self-determination (how I live my life) and co-determination (how we share life) go together. It's about being more conscious of how the world works and how and where our lives actually fit into it.

Mindfulness begins with being still and continues with being aware of the inner nudgings you experience throughout your life. Some also know this practice as prayer or meditation. For example, a friend of mine who's an artist grew up in a home that valued a certain level of education and a specific profession not related to art. She complied with what was expected of her to go to college and then graduate school and then started working in a profession that was actually chosen by her family, not her. As time passed, she found yourself tired, unenthused, even a bit angry, though she couldn't pinpoint why. She viewed her art as a hobby because that's what she was always told it was, and found herself longing for every second she could steal away from "real" life to do what she loved.

One day, a friend turned her on to a book about mindfulness, and she decided to take on the practice of meditation. She wasn't sure how to do it or if it would even work for her, but she decided to give it a try for just five minutes a day. Over time, she realized some pretty major shifts in the way she was responding to things on a daily basis. She wasn't yelling at cars during her traffic-filled commute. She didn't find herself writing furious draft emails to an annoying coworker that she'd eventually delete but needed a way to release the pressure. And life at home seemed less tense. She had more patience with her partner and kids. And she had more time for her artwork because she wasn't as tired physically or emotionally. As time with her art increased, so did her dreams of what she'd like to do with it, until one day she rented a space at the local flea market and sold her first piece. She and her life partner have worked out a transition plan that will eventually allow her to move from her current profession to her artwork full time without disrupting the financial security they both valued. Her mindfulness led her to the opportunity to flourish.

Man's Search For Meaning, the classic book by Viktor Frankl, helped me understand that there's actually a power within us that can't be taken away from us. From the lens of his life in the horrors of a concentration camp, he illustrates that everything can be taken from a person except one thing, the last of the human freedoms: to choose one's attitude in any set of circumstances — to choose one's own way of being in life. That is primarily about self-determination. It's about spending time wherever you need to spend it, so that you can gain clarity on the person you want to be and the way you want to show up in the world. Frankl also makes this observation:

> "Ever more people today have the means to live,
> but no meaning to live for."

This is perhaps the greatest gift that being "still" and developing a mindfulness practice has to offer: "meaning." When we spend time alone in stillness we get to know ourselves, which enables us to enter fully into relationships with others. This leads us to the next element, Core Relationships.

Core Relationships

The second element of human flourishing is Core Relationships. So many of us today feel lonely. One of the reasons we experience this ache, this absence of real communion with others, is that we do not have the kind of deep security and mutuality we need in our Core Relationships. These are the relationships you have with the People who you depend on, the People you support, and the People who support you. They include a Family of Choice, which we'll unpack a lot more later on. For now, consider that to companion others, you first need to companion yourself. It's super easy in our high-tech, fast-paced, phone-in-our-hands-at-all-times world to become so self-preoccupied, so self-centered and self-serving, that we begin to buy the illusion of independence. Developing a mindfulness practice helps us see through this illusion and equips us with the "soul tools" we need to discover the "meaning" in our relationships with our inner circle of People. Life Compass Living helps us give the most important People the best of what we have to offer. It helps us honor the "Yes" and "No" of both ourselves and our loved ones as we learn to love each other well, without projecting expectations upon one another.

Physical Vitality

Then there's *physical vitality*. In a delightful book called *Move Your DNA: Restore Your Health Through Natural Movement*, author Katy Bowman describes our need to use our bodies the way they were made to be used — the way they thrive. We were *not* created to sit in a chair for several hours a day. We were not even made to go through life with shoes and soft beds, if you can believe it! We certainly weren't made to live lives without movement, so physical activity is imperative. I did not modify my life in every way she suggested, but her point is valid and worth full consideration. If we continue to condition our bodies and keep moving, this is actually more of a determinant for overall vitality and well-being than your body mass index. We need to take responsibility for each part of our lifestyle that impacts our health and remember to stay physically active, using our bodies the way they were meant to be used.

We will decide how we care for ourselves in order to maintain our physical vitality. We will also find that our ability to care for ourselves is influenced by our People. We tend to get healthy together and the reverse. There are many ways we can join a group that supports a healthy lifestyle. Move, walk, run, dance, or join with others who share a life-giving practice that will positively impact your physical being, like yoga or water aerobics. Take some friends with you or make some friends when you arrive. In his book *Live Long, Die Short*, Roger Landry describes what we as the human race are discovering about maintaining vitality throughout our lives. Building longer lives of vitality is done through what and how much we eat, what we do to stay active, even if we don't run marathons, and how we manage the stresses of real life. My hope for all of us is that we help one another build and maintain physical vitality. I'm not advocating for a particular lifestyle. I'd just like to reiterate what science tells us — physical vitality is critical to reducing stress, increasing our resilience during times of stress, and significantly helping in the overall aging process.

Mental Vitality

And we can't forget *mental vitality*. There's much value in being a lifelong learner. We benefit greatly by continuing to learn. There used to be a belief that we all had a limited number of brain cells, and we had fewer as we continued the aging process. This reinforced a cultural notion that cognitive decline was as "natural" as physical decline. Now, we're learning that neither is true. Mentally speaking, we're discovering that our brain continues to rejuvenate itself, developing stem cells and new neural pathways through a process known as neuroplasticity.

The great news is we can do simple exercises that promote neuroplasticity, regardless of age. For example, ensuring we get enough sleep, adopting an exercise routine (especially aerobic exercise), reading, challenging ourselves to brain games, etc. Just Google "neuroplasticity exercises" and you'll be amazed at the variety of different ways you can stimulate the process. One of the most significant benefits of neuroplasticity is its buffer against dementia. Proactively engaging in activities that foster neuroplasticity allows us to actually exercise some power over what many have considered something we have no power over.

Even those who have been diagnosed with dementia can delay the progression of it. My sons enjoy reading fiction and that includes fantasy and science fiction. They said I was missing a lot and could benefit by doing the same. I maintained my practice of NOT reading much fiction. In my reading and research about how we can help ourselves stay vital in the brain and mind, I discovered that they were right. When we, by reading fiction, learn new languages and imagine the way life and relationships unfold in a world different than our own, we invigorate the organ of the brain and build the capacity of our minds to flow with the challenges and changes of real life. Who knew that Harry Potter, Frodo Baggins, and Katniss were also helping us as we joined them in their adventures? Learning a foreign language or a new activity, (sport, hobby, or artistic expression) will help as well.

Are active people more likely to enjoy learning? Yep. Are life-long learners more likely to stay active? Yep. It's a two for one. The two go hand in hand.

TWO BARRIERS TO FLOURISHING

As we continue to explore what it means to flourish, I want to directly address two lies that often get in our way. I hope they are less troublesome for you, but I have found them to be so rooted in my world view that I have to work daily to avoid their toxicity.

The first is the lie of the independent self.

As individuals, we may like to think that our security is a solo creation, and yet the independent self is really something that cannot exist. There will always be tension between individuality and togetherness. This is a classic problem. We want to own the responsibility of directing our own lives and yet we are part of the world and connected to the lives of others and the life of the Earth.

The more we can mindfully choose how to be in relationship with others, the more we will be able to share a life that honors and supports each of us and all the others we care about. The Life Compass protocol allows us to start where we are and with those closest to us and then expand into the community at large.

Sounds great, right? It is. However, relationships require hard work. There have definitely been plenty of times in my relationships when I've caught myself buying into the lie that living an independent life would be a heck of a lot easier. Just me, myself, and I, living in my own place — going to bed when *I* want to go to bed, getting up when *I* want to get up, listening to the music *I* want to listen to, watching what *I* want to watch on TV, putting the toilet paper roll on the way *I* want it. ... Ah, the fantasy of living independently can often be nothing less than pure bliss. Then I look at my wife while she's in our garden or one of my grandbabies taking a nap, and all of that goes away. This happens in all of our minds on days when living in relationship is hard. It's natural for us to want to escape conflict. The lie of the independent self tells us that if we maintain wealth and health, we can make sure we don't need others and will enjoy a life of complete freedom from being "needy" and dependent or even a burden. And we expect others to do the same. For some of us, the lie will also tell us that we can help the People we love without expecting anything in return. None of this is true. We were born to connect and share life. We were born to recognize and accept our humanity and the humanity of those we love. None of us will live our lives perfectly. Isn't that what grace is all about? The lie of the independent self contributes to anxiety, depression, loneliness, desolation, and resentment. We have to let go of our expectations so we can have authentic relationships. Reading this book means you are making an effort to flourish as yourself and share life well. It is worthy work for you and me as unique individuals writing our Life Stories. It is also the work that demonstrates the value of those we include in our Stories and our Plans. In this book, we will notice more of the resources and relationships that expose the independent self as a lie and help us end the isolation that keeps us lonely, scared, and trapped in the poverty of trying to live that lie.

The second is the lie of permanence.

Life does not unfold in a way that stays the same. Every place and everyone in those places is going through transitions. Many of these transitions have become traditions that serve us well. For example, I loved getting my driver's license, graduating high school, getting married, finding some fulfilling work, becoming a parent, and a host of other gifts wrapped up in the form of a transition. We don't need to criticize our hopes of experiencing a "normal" life that is predictable, secure, and satisfying. But we do need to criticize our inability to learn, grow, and adjust to life on life's terms. Life Compass Living is about helping one another find clarity and contentment while developing the ability to go with the flow of life's changes with a reduced level of anxiety.

As we work against these two lies, we are helping one another accept our need to support one another and embrace the reality of each life transition, including our final transition. Our denial of our need for each other and our inevitable deaths keeps us trapped in the lies of independence and permanence. Ernest Becker and some he influenced have studied and written about a concept called Terror Management Theory. In his Pulitzer Prize-winning book, *The Denial of Death*, he suggests we will live better lives if we accept the sheer terror of this fact: We're going to die. This is fairly obvious to some, but not everyone shares the insight. As we accept the impermanent nature of our existence, we can live fuller, richer lives with our legacy in mind. Yes, when we die, we will stop being part of events and conversations and fade from a starring role in the stories of our People, but we'll never cease to influence and to shape the world as time moves forward. The ripples of our living are eternal. That's a fact of living we can own and plan accordingly.

On the other side of these two lies, we will discover the truths about how we can flourish together. Life Compass Living is a tool that helps us do just that.

THE CHARTER FOR COMPASSION

I want to highlight that Life Compass Living is guided by the Charter for Compassion, a document urging the peoples and faith traditions of planet Earth to embrace the core value of compassion in mutuality. This

Charter has spread to more than 30 languages and has been endorsed by more than 2 million individuals around the globe.

As we were building the Life Compass model, I realized that the people we were working with did not all share a common faith tradition, nor a common way of shaping the ethics that inform our work and relationships. I decided that one thing we could share is *compassion*. For the Life Compass Living community to reach its potential, we will need to do the work of bringing genuine compassion to our conversations and plans. This includes compassion for ourselves.

Real life is messy and tenuous. If we are going to do relationships — especially if we are going to face off with the anxieties of building closer relationships — it will be messy and tenuous. But with the Life Compass Plan protocol, we are going to make this shared reality easier. As we bring compassion for ourselves and others to every conversation, we'll be able to be together, come alongside one another, meet our present needs and secure our shared future. As wisdom and compassion lead us, Life Compass Living can create a world for ourselves and others that gets us a little bit closer to our potential as we admit and embrace the fact that we are in this together. We will benefit ourselves even as we build a better world for our neighbors and future generations.

The Charter for Compassion reads as follows:

> *The principle of compassion lies at the heart of all religious, ethical and spiritual traditions, calling us always to treat all others as we wish to be treated ourselves. Compassion impels us to work tirelessly to alleviate the suffering of our fellow creatures, to dethrone ourselves from the centre of our world and put another there, and to honour the inviolable*

sanctity of every single human being, treating every-
body, without exception, with absolute justice, equity
and respect.

It is also necessary in both public and private life to
refrain consistently and empathically from inflicting
pain. To act or speak violently out of spite, chau-
vinism, or self-interest, to impoverish, exploit or
deny basic rights to anybody, and to incite hatred
by denigrating others — even our enemies — is a
denial of our common humanity. We acknowledge
that we have failed to live compassionately and that
some have even increased the sum of human misery
in the name of religion.

We therefore call upon all men and women to restore
compassion to the centre of morality and religion
— to return to the ancient principle that any inter-
pretation of scripture that breeds violence, hatred or
disdain is illegitimate — to ensure that youth are
given accurate and respectful information about
other traditions, religions and cultures — to encour-
age a positive appreciation of cultural and religious
diversity — to cultivate an informed empathy with
the suffering of all human beings — even those
regarded as enemies.

We urgently need to make compassion a clear, lumi-
nous and dynamic force in our polarized world.
Rooted in a principled determination to transcend

selfishness, compassion can break down political, dogmatic, ideological and religious boundaries. Born of our deep interdependence, compassion is essential to human relationships and to a fulfilled humanity. It is the path to enlightenment, and indispensable to the creation of a just economy and a peaceful global community.[3]

CHAPTER 2

Person

"We fear our highest possibility
(as well as our lowest one).
We are generally afraid to become that which we
can glimpse in our most perfect moments."
— Abraham Maslow

The Life Compass was designed for all adults, although most 18-year-olds won't see the value of imagining and planning for where they'll be when they're turning 60. There is, however, a common thread across all ages. Whether we realize it or not, we all want to direct our own lives and become the best version of ourselves we can be. Our best and true self is a potentiality we're born with, but it's up to us to build the relationships where that potential can come to fruition. Think of our mind, imagination, ability to love, natural talents, physical body, and core values as the tools in our tool box. They all afford us the unique opportunity to build and *live in* what's most important to us as individuals. This represents our "Person."

The things *most true* about us are like little diamonds waiting to be discovered and developed over time. They're there from the beginning and taking shape as we grow, but it takes some effort and self-mining for us to actually find and name them. Their greatest value, which is truly priceless, is the inner peace they provide us as they are brought to the surface of our conscious experience and allowed to bloom for all to see. Pause for a moment and think about a time in your life that you weren't in alignment with your true self and the values you cherish. Perhaps it was a time you lied about something (abandoning your source in truth), or didn't stick up for a friend or co-worker because you were afraid of what others would think (denying your truest harmony with compassion and loyalty). Maybe it was a job you chose to remain in despite your knowledge of the company's unethical or borderline illegal practices (betraying the integrity at your essence). How did you feel during those times? I have my stories and current challenges just like those.

This is an innate part of being human and growing up — even when you're 60 years old, like me. We are moving from being a child to an adult and need to make space for both. Some of my mentors point out the need for a "beginner's mind" even as they share their wisdom. There's an interesting word that's burst onto the scene recently, particularly among generational millennials. *Adulting.* It's when we decide to take on the responsibilities and decisions that come along with adulthood. I enjoy this word. Actually, I had to decide again today to keep adulting. We all do. It's more than simply a role or a stage —- it's a set of actions.

Not long ago, I saw a list of what it means to be a true adult. It came from Marc Chernoff, co-author of *Getting Back to Happy*. In his blog post, he reminds us that adulting is "an ongoing process, not a state" and listed 20 characteristics of being an adult. Here are some of them:

- Continuously striving for self-improvement.
- Being able to manage personal jealousy and feelings of envy.

- Demonstrating the ability to listen to and evaluate the viewpoints of others.
- Maintaining patience and flexibility on a daily basis.
- Accepting the fact that you can't always win, and learning from mistakes instead of whining about the outcome.
- Not over-analyzing negative points but instead looking for the positive points in the subject being analyzed.
- Knowing the difference between rational decision-making and emotional impulse.

While these are just a few highlights from one particular list, they all have something in common, don't they? They're each a purposeful and deliberate way of being that we discover and develop from our own unique center. In fact, when we've made a decision to do that thing called adulting, we've decided to be proactive as well. There's no sitting on the sidelines when it comes to adulting.

If you're reading this book, I believe that you've decided to either start or keep adulting. Congratulations! You've entered into the company of proactive people who want the best life possible, *and* who are willing to do the necessary work to make it a reality.

IDENTITY, VALUE, AND SIGNIFICANCE

One significant part of *adulting* is the willingness to share our Life Story and reflectively listen to the Life Stories of others. To do this, we need to keep a few aspects in mind. One is our identities, the second is our values, and the third is our ways of finding significance. The foundation for this framework originated from the school of family systems theory many know from Edwin Friedman and Murray Bowen. I found this framework incredibly helpful as I worked with my own counselors and spiritual directors over the years, and it's my goal to share with you the wisdom and insights I've gained through my experience. If you're considering seeing a counselor as part of your self-discovery journey, then I highly recommend seeing a professional who has been schooled in these theories. These folks hold deep clinical knowledge that can be greatly beneficial as you look to better understand yourself in relation to the family system you were born into. For more information on family systems theory, you'll find a list of resources in the bibliography. For the purposes of our discussion here and throughout the book, we'll use the three elements — our identity, values, and ways of finding significance — as the guardrails that will help us as we come to know ourselves and engage in our Essential Conversations.

Identity

Identity involves answering the question, "Who am I?" It's an ongoing process of re-consideration, reflection, and reframing that often changes depending on life's circumstances and the lessons we've learned from those circumstances. We spend our lives seeking to define ourselves both as individuals and who we are as individuals within a group of People. We then weave what we've discovered into stories that we tell ourselves and the world. My most common struggle when it comes to identity is differentiation. What I mean by that, and what I'm sure many can relate to, is the incredible challenge of not allowing the emotions, demands, and expectations of others to consume me. This wrestling with differentiation (I am me and you are you) is something that starts in early childhood, and in my experience has been helped by my spiritual practice, therapists and spiritual directors. I've spent countless hours focused on this struggle in my mindfulness practices, reflective journaling, and conversations with trusted friends. I continue to consistently and repeatedly answer the question, *"Who am I?" and "How do I want to be known in the world?"*

I believe that as we own an identity, a version of ourselves (for example, "George 2.0"), we're better able to shape a vision for our best selves, our true selves. Think of the words "best" and "true" as the ultimate goals. We will never fully know and become our "best" and "true" selves, but we can make incremental progress. As they say in Alcoholics Anonymous, we seek progress not perfection. To do this, we start with authenticity. When we're "real" with ourselves and others, there's an inherent peace that follows; our anxiety, depression, and the longing to be living as someone else vanishes. Instead of living as our "stage characters" (another gold nugget from AA), we're able to walk comfortably in our own skin. I'm grateful for all who have helped me learn to spend more time living as "George," singing my own songs, and loving others with less manipulation while continuing to love myself. Don't worry about getting it right. Focus on finding and sharing what you learn about the wonderful self that resides in you. You are worth the work of being discovered and set free to flourish!

Value

While it is my privilege, my responsibility, and my job to decide who I am as an individual, I also need to identify and operate out of a set of core *values*. Life is about the things we assign value and importance. Values, priorities, and character traits guide the way we live.

> Focus on finding and sharing what you learn about the wonderful self that resides in you. You are worth the work of being discovered and set free to flourish!

Most of us know all too well what our parents, society, and culture at large think we *should* value, but we really haven't spent much time identifying what *we* value. Instead, we tend to inadvertently stumble upon our values. For example, we hear from one friend information that we told another friend in confidence. Ouch. That hurt. Why did that hurt? Because we value confidentiality and trust. We lay awake at night worrying about how we'll pay our bills. Why? Because we value integrity and our credit score. Our values give our lives meaning and ease our existential angst centering around *why* we're alive.

British author and motivational speaker Simon Sinek wrote a book called *Start With Why.* He suggests that we start with *why* and then move to *how*, and next to *what*. Along the same lines, German philosopher Friedrich Wilhelm Nietzsche is quoted as saying, "A man will endure any *how*, provided he knows the *why*." This emphasis on *why* is profoundly true. We need to allow ourselves the time to become clear on our values: the *whys* of our existence, the People who are important to us, the guideposts of our journeys. There's a plethora of material available online that can guide you through discovering your core values. If you really want to do a deep dive, I recommend considering a few life coaching sessions, finding a counselor you trust, or letting a spiritual director help you mine the riches of your faith tradition. The clearer you are on your values, the better equipped you'll be to direct your own life and stick to those values as you choose to share your life with others.

Significance

The third element is *significance,* the *what* and the *how* of life. What is it you're going to do with your life, and then how will you do it? As the fabulous poet Mary Oliver asks, "What will you do with your one wild and precious life?" Significance is important. It's about purpose. It's about the difference you make in the world. It is having clarity on the plot that guides your Life Story and how you will act out that story with the rest of us. As the journey unfolds, sometimes our path remains a fairly straight line and other times it takes a radical turn or two. We've all seen people — perhaps you're one of them — make major life shifts. This is all part of the process of continuously following the love, losses, lessons, and longings that feed our hunger for significance. These life experiences also enable us to develop a larger perspective on the world and create the aspects of the legacy we'll leave for generations to come.

If you haven't already, start writing down the things you want to do and how you want to do them. It's time to get intentional about how and with whom we spend our time and where we invest our energy. Time is a priceless gift. It is also one of life's greatest equalizers. Not only is it priceless, it's also one of life's greatest equalizers. It defies race, religion, socioeconomic status, sexual orientation, and every other label out there. No matter how wealthy you are, you can't buy more time. No matter how intelligent or crafty you are, you can't stop or turn back the clock. Unfortunately, many of us don't realize this truth until it's too late. As the psalmist said, "Teach us, Oh Lord, to number our days so that we may gain hearts of wisdom." (Psalm 90). Keeping the reality that our time is limited in the forefront of our minds helps us create significance.

Some of my most precious moments are spent with my wife during our annual weekend getaway. We carve out time at the end of every year to rest and reflect on what worked for us individually and as a couple, and what didn't. Part of this process includes our calendar. With the time we have remaining after our commitments to ourselves, our kids and grandkids, and work, we then decide where and with whom we'll spend our time during the coming year. This helps us ensure we're spending it wisely. As an extrovert, it's super important that I honor my wife's introversion and need to recharge alone. Likewise, it's just as important for her to honor my need to be with people. Intentionally deciding what social events we'll attend together or I'll attend solo is a critical part of both of us flourishing as individuals and in our relationship. To prioritize my days, I use the system David Allen mapped out in his book *Getting Things Done*. You may see this as a time management system, and that is fine as well. I've had friends find other tools helpful. Do whatever works for you. My biggest hope is that you'll identify and work to align your time with the priorities that spark meaning in every aspect of your being. For our souls to dance, we must choreograph each step.

THE LIFE STORY MODEL

One tool I've found incredibly helpful when it comes to discovering and developing our evolving *identity, value,* and *significance* is the **Life Story Model**. Have you ever thought of your life as a story with you as the Author? It's true that we don't have control over every incident that happens in our lives, but we actually have more say in *how the story goes* than we may think. Each element of the model empowers us to better frame our own Life Story, so that we can, first and foremost, be the Author of it and, secondly, be better equipped to share it with others.

This model is truly about self-determination, and its magic allows us to better choose the way we live our lives, no matter what real life brings our way. Before going any further, it's important to understand that you not only have the right to your own Life Story but you're actually responsible for it — for your sake and the sake of those you love.

Dan P. McAdams of Northwestern University has developed a more expanded version of the science, history, and understanding of the Life Story Model. I've simplified it to make it accessible for use in our Essential Conversations. Dan is one of the voices that encourages us all to direct the story of our lives and to build "affirming narratives of interpersonal communion."[4]

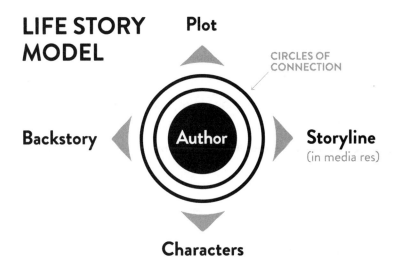

LIFE STORY MODEL

Plot

CIRCLES OF CONNECTION

Backstory

Author

Storyline
(in media res)

Characters

The first element of the Life Story is the *Author*. Recognizing that *we're* the Author of our story is one of the biggest challenges we face. Many of us have been taken over to one degree or another by dysfunctional relationships — so much so that we can barely see past the chaos in our daily lives to think about anything except survival. Often, the dysfunction started in the family where we began life. As we've grown through the years, the dysfunction has accumulated in layers like an onion. For a variety of reasons, we've surrendered the Author role, most of us not even realizing the role exists. Shame. Guilt. Low self-esteem. Fear. Trauma. Rage. Fighting to protect ourselves in an abusive environment. These are just a few of the thieves that steal this birthright. Others of us have had supportive families and still find that our culture puts pressure on us to become dutiful consumers and follow the marching orders we are given. I wholeheartedly believe that it's a lifelong task to keep re-owning our role as Author. If we claim this mantle in each season of our lives, the practice of this first element will make all the difference.

If the idea of being the Author of your own Life Story sparks a bit of energy in you — that's exactly what it's intended to do. It comes from a place of power and creativity that each of us are born with. We're innately designed with a magnificent brain that allows us to think in symbols and then actually build what we've imagined. We can see something in our mind's eye and then make it a reality. This is truly powerful stuff. The great news is you can begin embracing the authorship of your Life Story today, regardless of age or life situation. As you put yourself in the story, start focusing on being authentic and relying less on the stage characters you've created, those versions of yourself that only serve your anxieties and the agendas of others.

Starting now, let your "yes" mean "yes" and your "no" mean "no." This is challenging, I know. Many of us are "people pleasers" and are driven to be "liked." We don't want to hurt the feelings of others by saying "no." If we do, they may reject us. This is a very simplified description of what professionals call codependency. Others of us build walls around our hearts in an attempt to protect ourselves from vulnerability. Instead of being quick to say "yes," we're quick to say "no," which ultimately leads us to push people away. This is a very simplified description of commitment phobia. Pause for a moment and think this through. Who are you ultimately harming when you aren't speaking your truth? That's right. You. If it's easier to acquiesce to the request (or demand) of others than to face the anxiety that comes up when setting a clear boundary — or if it's easier to completely dismiss the possibility of developing a relationship past a certain point, or completely "disappear" from one that's passed a certain point — then you're well on your way to developing serious chronic health conditions (if you haven't already). These scenarios are flip sides of the same fear of rejection, and both are harmful emotionally and physically. Taking ownership of your Life Story empowers you to live from a place of trust instead of fear. It's absolutely possible to get to a point in your life where setting boundaries becomes easier. We can never set perfect boundaries, but we can become better at it if we stay awake and consistently work on it each and every time the need to set one appears. If you're not sure where to start, start here: "Now isn't a good time for me but I so appreciate the invitation. Let's see where I am next time around" (for those battling codependency). Or. "I'm feeling a little nervous in our relationship and want to make sure we're on the same page. I'd love to hear where you think we are" (for those struggling with commitment phobia). Owning our role as the Author of our own Life Story is the first step toward being true to our healthy selves. Fuller authorship, no pun intended, of your Life Story will grant the joy and responsibility of being truly alive.

The second element is the *Plot,* which basically translates to the chapters of your story within a larger story. You'll notice that what I'm about to say is something that I will say numerous times, in different ways, because it can't be overstated. *As humans, we were created to live in community.* Every spiritual teacher in every tradition has told us we can't be ourselves without being a part of something bigger than ourselves. If we are left alone too long, we die. With this in mind, I want you to think about the larger stories with which your individual Life Story has been woven. For example, a family, religion, philosophy, community, or other network of relationships. What impact have these larger stories had on your life? Are they fueling your passion or draining you? Is the narrative "done" or is there more that you are to gain or contribute (or both) by continuing your dance with a particular larger story? If you're not sure either way — that's OK. You're at least growing in your awareness. If the purpose of your connection to a particular community is complete, what's keeping you there? As a pastor, I've met many individuals who were raised in a particular religious denomination or religion that did not feed their soul, and yet they stayed there year after year because they were too scared of what others would think if they made a move to a different spiritual tradition. I've also met many individuals who needed to disengage from their family of origin because of generational toxicity but feared the grief and sadness this would bring up in them. Instead of setting healthy boundaries with their blood relatives and choosing to *create* a family with emotionally healthy people, they remained in the familiar swirl of chaotic and poisonous energy they'd known since birth. Their fear told them a dysfunctional family was better than no family at all. Others I've known have struggled with the consequences of their kids getting sucked into the wrong larger story (aka "crowd"). They've paid big price tags for attorneys, replacing totaled cars, drug treatment programs, and more.

The reality is the moment we receive our life it begins unfolding alongside the lives of others. As you become the Author of your story, you have the opportunity to intentionally choose which larger stories you "belong" to. Trust yourself. There is deep wisdom within you waiting to be discovered, but it can be easily missed. Oftentimes, it comes in the form of a whisper. Pay close attention. These whispers may call you to get quiet and listen with the help of others you trust. My experience is that I have to create the space and time away from the noise and busyness of life to hear the voice of, see the shape of, and choose the way of my best self. It seems a lot like the need to be in the space where I sit now as I write this book. We are not helped by the chatter of all those who want us to conform to their agendas. This work of choosing your life is not a selfish act. **It is good to choose how and why we live so death just hands the completed magnum opus to all who will assess and remember the way we guided the story that is ours to write.** As Steven Pressfield says in *The War of Art*, "It's a gift to the world and every being in it. Don't cheat us of your contribution. Give us what you've got!"[5]

The next element is the *Characters*. When you start reading a novel that grabs you from the start and keeps you wanting more at the end, one of the things you'll most likely discover is the painstaking effort the author puts into character development. It's the characters — the People — that captivate you. If we want to do what is best for ourselves, we cannot do it alone. However, the People in our lives will come and go. Some will stay. As we get to know the People in our lives and have our Essential

Conversations, we will be better able to decide together how the story unfolds for the good of us all.

Take a look at the People in your life and remember that you don't have to keep the same characters in your story. It can be challenging to decide who will be in our Life Story and how they will be included, but it's definitely worth the effort. Thankfully, with the help of mentors, friends, counselors, spiritual directors, and the University of Real Life, I am developing one of my biggest and most valuable life disciplines — the ability to give myself permission to decide *how* someone fits in my life, if at all.

I was glad to learn that we do not have to stop caring to stop being codependent. We do not have to *play along* every time we play with others. We can be solid, compassionate and wise. That's how we find a better way, change the rules we follow, and heal one another. The next element is a big part of how we become solid, compassionate, and wise.

All stories start somewhere and include a *Backstory*. Authors tell you enough about the backstory to explain what is occurring in the story and where it is headed. Counselors often have you revisit your childhood because it's filled with a plethora of information about how you were taught to relate to yourself and share life with others. As children, we created patterns of relating that are imprinted in our subconscious beings and form the "roles" we often play and the rules we follow in our relationships. Some of what we learned growing up serves us well in life. We can find things to be grateful for that help us relate well, and affirm our value and the value of others. But we all have some negative patterns that were handed to us early and may have become more entrenched along the way. Have you ever said or heard someone else say, she or he's "got some serious baggage"? Well, that's what this is.

What we find in the baggage and blessings of our past becomes our "backstory." As we take on the role of Author, it becomes our responsibility to deal with our baggage. We may have more baggage than some and less than others. Let's find the help we need to accept the baggage that is part of your backstory and learn to incorporate it in a Life Story of our choosing.

When we own our backstory and change the trajectory of our storyline, tension will emerge. It is hard work. As you become more aware of your backstory and its place in your overall Life Story, your clarity about which characters will continue to play a part will sharpen. As the Author, you decide what you learn from, what you depend on, and what you take from your backstory. You may be thinking. "George, my (mother, father, sister, brother, aunt, uncle, mother-in-law, father-in-law, etc. — fill in the blank) is not healthy, but I can't just write (him/her) out of my Life Story." I understand. This is a universal challenge we all face. Actually, some of us have tried to completely erase certain characters from our story — and we may even think we've succeeded — but the reality is it's not possible.

Please note: We can physically leave a relationship that is causing physical, emotional, sexual, and/or spiritual harm. You may need to leave. Immediately. My point is, there's no way to completely cut a character out of our lives without taking care of the baggage that resulted from our relationship with that character. The baggage will continue to show up in our backstory and negatively impact our current relationships until we get the help we need and do the work that enables us to choose how to take responsibility for our lives. We all carry scars on our hearts. Scars are signs of hurt and healing. They never go away completely, which is actually a good thing. Scars remind us of where we've been, what we need to avoid in the future, and our resilience. We can be grateful for the good memories and supportive relationships. We can also grow from the painful lessons learned from the unhealthy times in our relationships, including the ones we made ourselves. When we leave behind the items that we've carried from childhood that no longer serve the life we want to live, it makes room for new insights and opportunities for deeper, richer relationships. In time, we'll develop the capacity and wisdom to choose which of our old characters stay, which new characters we'll invite in, and how all of them will participate in our story as it continues to unfold.

Next, we move to the actual *Storyline*. How does it all unfold? If you're guided by the Plot, if you've decided which characters are part of your story, if you've done what you need to with the backstory so that you can arrive in the present moment, how will you move forward? This is your storyline. How is it going to go from here?

Full authorship of your Life Story will grant the joy and responsibility of being truly alive.

One of the things we seek is happiness ... I like reading some of the work of positive psychology. There's a book by Shawn Achor called *The Happiness Advantage*. It's one of the books that's helpful for defining and finding happiness. As we're collectively learning more about happiness, there's evidence that *being* happy has a lot to do with *choosing* to be happy. We're also realizing that happiness in the short term is not as important as overall contentment with, and happiness about, how our lives are going. Achor says, "For me, happiness is the joy we feel striving after our potential."[6] May that be at least one of the storylines for all of our lives.

In the above diagram, one of the things you'll notice under Storyline is the words "in medias res." When I was telling my son, who was an English Literature major, about the Life Story Model, he mentioned *in medias res*. In medias res points to the things that enter a narrative without preamble, a character who arrives right in the middle of things. Real life is never neat, it's never exactly "right." If you think about it, the books you don't believe are the ones that are too neat, where characters are way too narrow. We like the reality of messiness, because it fits the reality we know. Our storylines unfold in medias res, in the middle of things. As each person enters our story and we enter theirs, it is helpful to remember you are both starting in medias res. I find it very helpful to slow down all my conclusions about a person I am meeting or getting to know better. It helps me remember that I can choose how I introduce myself to people so that I can start our relationships with the open, gracious, and curious qualities that are more like an author doing research for his or her book. The Life Stories of real people will be messy and tenuous, even while they strive to live out plot lines of noble intent. This is why compassion toward others and ourselves must be our constant guide as our stories unfold.

The final element of the Life Story diagram above is *Circles of Connection*. We'll use this element to focus our attention on ensuring our relationships are in harmony with their importance to our lives. The deepest *center circle* is the one with ourselves as the Author of our Life Story. The circles that expand from there are the Circles of Connection. This visual is a way to think about how the characters in our Life Story will take shape. The most essential group of People in your Life Story are the People closest to the center of the Circles of Connection. Those are the People we depend on and those who depend on us. I'll describe this in detail in the next chapter, plus unveil a process that will help you locate People in your Circles of Connection. As you work through the process, you will determine who you want to share life with and how to create a shared life that is more secure and enables everyone to flourish. It will be work, but there will be plenty of joy as well.

THE DIGNITY OF CHOICE

Now that we've stepped into the Author role of our Life Story, it's equally important that we respect the right of every person we know to be the Author of their own Life Story. Every person has the choice, power, and responsibility to determine who they are as an individual, what their values are, and how they find significance in this world. Honoring this reality is what we call Dignity of Choice, and it's critical to living in alignment with our Life Compass and respecting the Life Compass of those we love. This trait was driven home for me on a slide I saw in a presentation at an elder law conference that took place in Vancouver, BC, Canada.

The presenter displayed a slide containing two images. On the left side was a picture of a young man. He looked like he was in his 20s, and rock climbing. From my point of view, it appeared as if he was holding onto the edge of a cliff, on the verge of falling. He needed to scale onto a level place to stand, but was precariously hanging over the ledge. The image on the right side of the slide was of an older gentleman who was working hard to climb the stairs in a house. The question the presenter asked is one that's stuck with me ever since: "Who," she asked, "do you admire the most?"

It arrested me in a powerful way. Initially, I thought I admired the young man more. He was on an adventure, climbing a rock. I suppose that I saw the older gentleman as someone taking a risk, maybe an *unnecessary* risk of falling, because it looked like he was struggling to get up the steps. Eventually, I realized that was simply ageism. I then allowed myself to wonder:

"What if that young man had preschool children at home? What if that young man's family depended on his income? Did he have insurance or a financial plan that would secure their future if he fell on his climb? Was the thrill he was seeking worth the risk he was taking? Was he one fall away from causing huge hardship on those who depended on him?"

And …

"What if that older gentleman just wanted to climb the steps to the room he had been sleeping in for 40 years, and he decided that it was worth the risk in order to remain in charge of his life? What if all his children were secure adults and his estate plan was set up to fund the education or professional training needed by his grandchildren?"

I didn't know if either was acting foolishly. Perhaps they both had all their plans in place to mitigate the risks of their climbs. My point is, there's a subtle yet powerful shift in thinking that occurs when we're living in harmony with all aspects of our Life Compass and give each person we care about the Dignity of Choice to define and express their own Life Compass. Self-determination is perhaps the place we begin to be human. It is certainly necessary to flourish as humans, and we will repel or resent those who try and take it away from us. In the Life Compass Living community, we will let the Golden Rule apply to the Dignity of Choice.

> Self-determination is perhaps the place we begin to be human. It is certainly necessary to flourish as humans, and we will repel or resent those who try and take it away from us.

This all sounds great in theory, but honoring someone's Dignity of Choice isn't easy. A dear friend recently confided that she was struggling with honoring her dad's Dignity of Choice. Her dad, age 77, has coronary artery disease and already had received three heart stents to clear blockages. Her sister called one day and said her father had been experiencing pressure in his chest and jaw when walking and that the sensation had been occurring intermittently for about a week. He wasn't willing to go to the ER. In fact, he refused to go, despite the pleadings of his wife, two daughters, and a trusted friend from church. Instead, he wanted to wait and see his cardiologist. This was very frustrating to everyone, including her father, who felt he knew his body better than anyone else.

My friend told her dad that she loved him very much and would also be very angry if he had a heart attack at home. He and his wife had already faced the tragic death of their son to an accidental overdose in their house, and the last thing his wife needed was the trauma of him potentially dying from a heart attack there. As hard as it was, my friend lovingly spoke her truth. She then spent time talking with her trusted circle about her anger and fear. Fortunately, her father made it to the cardiologist appointment and was admitted to the hospital the next day for triple bypass surgery.

This is a real-life example of honoring someone's Dignity of Choice. My friend didn't stuff her anger or fear, and she expressed her love. The outcome was not what she would have chosen for herself or her father, but it was ultimately his choice.

Dignity of Choice also includes other elements that make life rich and complex — one is the choice of who we love. Sometimes, this includes entering into a life partnership. After years of being married myself and working with hundreds of folks in committed relationships, I've come to realize that even the best life partnerships can be a happy, pretty mess. The good news is, with a Life Compass Plan, they can become a lot less messy and become — dare we say — "elegant."

I continue to treasure the encouragement I received from a woman who was participating in a Life Compass Living group in Chicago. I was invited to join one of the group sessions via a video conference to answer questions and talk about the insights the group was gaining. One of the female group participants said, "George, I'm so grateful for the Life Compass. I'm having some of the most mature conversations I've ever had with my husband. It's easy to love someone who supports your Life Compass." Yes! That's exactly the outcome I was hoping for. More than anything, I want to affirm our right to choose who we love and help us all have well-functioning relationships, where we secure the present and the future together.

An extension of honoring the Dignity of Choice is discovering and coming to accept the perspectives and passions of others. We often form unrealistic expectations based on how we see their lives, forgetting that they can only be who they are, know what they know, and have what they have in the moment. Open, honest conversations become a "must have" in order for us to truly understand and be understood. We must become lifelong learners so we can continue to discover not only the reality we live in — the story we tell ourselves — but the reality others live in, and the stories they are telling *themselves*. This is most important with those who are closest to us. All of us are figuring things out as we move along life's path.

This truth couldn't be more evident than in parenting. I see interpersonal artistry on display in the birthing of babies and raising children. When we do this, we share a journey as parents and children that we have very little idea how to do. And yet we do it, and this path often *becomes sacred work* done well. Anyone who has been a parent or has been parented knows that it's literally "on-the-job training." We can read the best books on the subject and still not be fully prepared. I want to honor this and other ways we make valiant efforts at nurturing ourselves and others. As part of this honoring, it's important to recognize that not everyone possesses the same instinct to nurture. Likewise, some who seek to nurture don't realize that the way they're choosing to pour themselves into others is unwise. Part of Life Compass Living is learning how to nurture ourselves and others in a healthy, life-giving way. Discernment is called for, of course, but the calling itself is beautiful and worthy of regard. A virtue that philosophers have prized for millennia is *mastery*. There are some people who have a calling, a compulsion to be really good at something, to be among the *best* at something. And they pay a price for this mastery; the people in their life also pay a price. Mastery is truly choosing something that is difficult but doable and then laser focusing on "taking it on." This is such an important aspect of our shared humanity. A Life Compass Plan facilitates mastery of our relationships, even while it embraces the imperfect realities they include.

THE OVERVIEW EFFECT

In addition to understanding our relationship to ourselves and others, I believe it's incredibly important for us to understand our relationship to the Earth — to the life of our biosphere. I remember reading about the experience of astronauts when they get outside of the planet's atmosphere and look down on the Earth. They experience a phenomenon called *the overview effect,* an interesting shift that occurs in their perception. They see that this place where we live —- full of complexity and conflict and heartache and joy —- is one organism; all the places and things we experience standing within our limited views are actually one full reality, one diverse and coordinated dance. I think it's vital for us to begin to understand, in deeper and bigger ways, the complexities of how our lives — our consumption, and our planetary interactions — impact not only the capacities for People to live well today, but the shared future of humanity that we are shaping with each choice we make.

PERSON SUMMARY

Throughout this chapter, we've explored at a very high level the importance of understanding our Person — our *identity, value,* and *significance.* We've talked about the responsibility of determining who we are as individuals, understanding both the positive and negative imprints from our family of origin, and what we need to do to address our baggage. We've also focused on the concept of becoming the Author of our Life Story and our commitment to respecting the right of every person we know to be the Author of their own Life Story.

The work we do on ourselves will be an ongoing journey, and there will be challenging times for sure. The great news is that every step we take toward discovering and becoming our better selves will only bring us that much closer to our full potential. We can't do it alone, though, which is a beautiful segue to the next chapter and second element of the Life Compass — People.

CHAPTER 3

People

"The degree of social connection that can improve our health and our happiness, as well as the daily experience of everyone who comes in contact with us, is both as simple and as difficult as being open and available to others."
— *John T. Cacioppo & William Patrick*

No matter how hard we try, there's no escaping people or relationships. We're all in this together and we're all deeply connected. If you study quantum physics, even at a basic level, you'll come to find that we're all made up of the same energy, and that energy is incredibly powerful. Most of us don't realize that our words, thoughts, emotions, and actions send ripples of vibrational energy that have a far-reaching effect — both positive and negative — on ourselves and others. That energy is what ties us together as part of the human family.

In the book *Lost Connections*, Johann Hari makes the observation that we're in the first period of human history where we're deconstructing our tribes or our support systems. We're finding more ways to socially connect, and losing touch with ways to deeply connect. Over time, we've subtly shifted to asking our children *what* they want to be versus *who* they want to be. Instead of asking them to reference who they are in relation to other people — their family, their teachers, their friends, their world — we ask *what* they're going to be in terms of economics and where they fit into productivity. Now, our message to our kids early on goes something like this:

"What you need to focus on as you develop your 'self' is how you're going to earn money and produce something that our culture values from a currency perspective. The people who are the most responsible are the people who are financially responsible."

When our sole focus is on the "what" rather than the "why" and "who," we inadvertently miss teaching our kids the responsibility of developing and maintaining deep, rich relationships, some that will last a lifetime. We turn their attention away from the sweet and beautiful experience of vulnerability and the gift of needing and being needed. We miss the opportunity to teach them how to experience the ultimate vibrancy of humanity in mutually dependent relationships. And we all know too well that relationships can be damaged and even destroyed when there's a primary focus on finances.

I believe that living well with others is not only the way to secure our lives in the present and in the future; I believe it's an essential part of how we reach our potential individually.

To regain what we've lost through *current, currency, community crisis,* and *constant change,* I believe we have to first acknowledge that we have a growing crisis in our relationships, an epidemic of health issues caused by lifestyle choices, and more emotional suffering even while the wealth of the developing world continues to grow. **It turns out that the world we are in is not the problem. It is the way we share the world we are in. I**

would like to suggest that we make it a priority to invest in our relationships. My hope is that this chapter will encourage you, no matter how old you are — whether you're entering adulthood or you've been there for decades. You have a fresh opportunity to rethink your life in terms of the challenge of being an adult who chooses how to relate, not only to yourself but to the people in your life, and most importantly, those who comprise your Core Relationships, which we will unpack next.

CIRCLES OF CONNECTION

I mentioned them in Chapter 2 and now I'd like to fully introduce what I call *Circles of Connection.* In the context of your Life Story, this becomes one tool for sorting out your characters. A Circle of Connection provides a framework for managing expectations, roles and resources on an emotional and practical level. It also helps define who you are in relation to others and your world.

In these Circles of Connection, you are the center-most sphere. Each Person who comes into your life is in their own Life Story and is now also in a relationship with you. As you develop your ability to own your personal responsibility, you are better able to work with your People to create an elegant plan for how to live, grow, and share life in a way that honors both your individual Life Stories and the story you're creating together.

As we move just slightly outward, we expand to include our most intimate relationships, the ones that matter the most, the ones that are the most practically and emotionally impactful in our lives — these are our Core Relationships. Continuing to move out from there, we recognize those who are not as intimate, not as significant, but yet are part of our lives. There are people on the outer bounds of these Circles of Connection who may be part of our lives for only a short time, and yet are very significant. For example, a nurse or therapist or someone else who is fulfilling a contract to provide services during a time of need.

RESPONSIBLE 'TO' VS. RESPONSIBLE 'FOR'

One distinction I'd like to make as we start talking about the ways we're connected to one another is between being responsible *to* someone and being responsible *for* someone. Ultimately, we're only responsible *for* ourselves and our children (until they reach a certain age or unless, of course, they are disabled in some way). As you begin thinking about the people in your life, it's worth recognizing that there may be people outside of minor or disabled children who you *choose* to be responsible for, and there may come a time when you need people to choose to be responsible for you. You certainly did when you began life. I remember holding each of my sons when they were born, recognizing my responsibility, and having some overwhelming emotions in response: they were totally dependent on me and my wife, Tammy, to provide for all their needs. They couldn't hold their heads up, feed themselves, keep themselves clean. They had no mobility. And yet we were celebrating. **We were celebrating the reality that this one who we held was to be loved by us and cared for by us.** As they grew up, I would actually have lively negotiations with them about the scope and limits of my responsibility. If that sounds strange to you, then I'm willing to be strange. But I would have conversations with my sons beginning somewhere around age 8, about being responsible for them and being responsible to them. I gave them the good and the bad news: The fact is that, until they were 18, I would be responsible for them at some level. But I understood their desire to have this decrease; I made it plain that this would indeed be the reality.

I would put one hand high and one hand low between us as we talked, and I would let my right hand descend and my left hand ascend, and I would say, "As my right hand is going down, I will be less and less responsible for you, and you will become, as my left hand rises, more and more responsible for yourself. And as they pass in the middle, in this time we call adolescence, there will probably be a lot of conflict, because we'll constantly be negotiating how I'm responsible as a parent to inform you, educate you, discipline you, and do the best job possible as a parent of someone who is taking responsibility for their own lives." Adulting was a great adventure we shared. I certainly matured as I stumbled along in my role as a parent.

This may seem ridiculous, but it front-loaded a basic truth that often takes parents and children by surprise (even though it happens all the time!). When we are in committed relationships, it is helpful to only take responsibility *for* another person when it is necessary and part of the role you have in their lives. **We can be responsible *to* one another in many ways without challenging personal responsibility and the Dignity of Choice.**

An article in the New York Post, titled "You're not an adult until you turn 24, science says" from January 20, 2018, observed that adulthood today begins at age 24. While we still define adolescence as happening between ages 10 and 19 — from the beginning of puberty until we cease biological growth — the reality is that people are taking on adulthood later. It is an understandable choice when you have no reason to think that the economy will make your work life stable, you don't trust serious relationships to go any better than they did for your parents, and you're staying more dependent on your parents because of college debt and the rising cost of living. I hear people making observations about how young adults don't *want* to grow up. I believe they would love to have the paths to adulthood that were available to my generation. It seems I failed, in some significant ways, to equip my children for the world, created by my generation, that was unraveling. I know I struggle to stay current with the tools coming online that are changing the way humans communicate, work, and share the earth. I hope Life Compass Living can help us all do some adulting together. When we are responsible *for* ourselves and *to* one another, we can learn to share the resources that secure our lives and enable us to flourish.

I chose to be responsible *to* Tammy as her husband at a gathering in Okemah, OK, on December 28, 1978. Since our wedding, there have been times in our relationship when she became sick, and it was very appropriate for me to choose to be responsible *for* her to some degree. Yet, most of the time over our 42 years together, she has made it crystal clear that I am responsible *to* her as her husband and someone who deeply loves her, but I am not responsible *for* her. This reminder typically comes when I'm attempting to fix something that she hasn't asked me to fix. I'm deeply grateful for the lessons she's taught me about negotiating and setting boundaries — with her, our children, those we love and, in one way or another, with everybody on Earth.

I remember joining a team of people to go and rebuild homes after Hurricane Katrina along the U.S. Gulf Coast back in 2005. It was amazing to see how many people made the journey to help strangers in need. By following the prompting of compassion, I brought these people into my Circles of Connection and was deeply blessed by our shared humanity. I wasn't responsible *for* them but I honored my responsibility *to* them as fellow humans. There is a progression of maturity and personal responsibility that is only possible when we combine it with a progression of compassionate and interdependent living. These may appear to be two paths to the life we want but they are actually realized in concert with one another.

It's hard work to make the counter-cultural choice to transition from viewing finances as our most valuable resource to viewing our relationships as our most valuable resource, but it's worth it.

At the center of our Circles of Connection are the smaller circles that have fewer people in them. These are the people we choose to be more responsible for in times when it's appropriate. By going through this process, you'll be able to intentionally choose the relationships you want and determine how you will invest in them from an emotional, physical, time, and financial standpoint. It's hard work to make the counter-cultural choice to transition from viewing finances as our most valuable resource to viewing our relationships as our most valuable resource, but it's worth it. It's important to do so, though, because humans are actually secure when we're relationally secure. We are actually vulnerable, and incapable of experiencing full human flourishing, when we are not in relationship to others in the ways that fully support our lives.

I remember one precious woman, I'll call her Meghan, who was in her 50s and single, never married, without children. She had a profession she loved in health care and was active in a faith community. She attended my Life Compass Living seminar and sought me out afterward to talk. Her family of origin lived in another community, and she didn't know if her friends could or would become part of her Family of Choice. She said, "I love my life and I don't feel any desire to make big changes, but now I see I need a plan for when I have to slow down or have a health crisis. I'm grateful that I'm thinking about this now, but I am afraid. I'll have the money I need, but I want more than professional support. Where should I start?"

She worked through her Life Compass Plan with all she had in her life at that time, and her fears began to subside. Over the next few months, we worked on her Life Story together, discussing where she wanted it to unfold and who she wanted to include. She even began to identify the legacy she hoped to leave. We mapped out some Essential Conversations for her to begin having with her family and a few friends.

Meghan saw me at a gathering several months after she committed to having those Essential Conversations. She walked toward me briskly and beaming! "George! You will be so glad to know I talked with my sister and my close friends. They were happy to know about my life choices, and we put some plans together like you suggested. I'm working with an attorney and setting up everything now. I'm staying here but I'm going to make visits back home so we can stay close and I can get to know my nephews and their children. A few of my friends have become more like family, and they're starting to have their own Essential Conversations. The Life Compass model has definitely changed my life!"

Knowing that we are not alone in our lives and vulnerabilities today, and will not be alone in our future lives and vulnerabilities, changes how our brains, our neurotransmitters, and our hormonal reflexes work. Indeed, this assurance not only makes it possible for us to live longer, but it enables us to experience more contentment, joy, and happiness in the days that we live.

Remember, in order to live a life that's focused on developing and investing in your relationships, it's imperative that you practice mindfulness and self-observation. You must make the time to define yourself as a Person and consistently strive to be the best version of yourself you can be. When we're stuck and unable to do this important work, it's good for us to go back and look again at our Life Story and find the help that we need in time alone, in time reflecting, in time in our spiritual practices, in time with a counselor or life coach. To have the capacity to own our Life Story, we must be clear on where we want our Life Story to go, so we can intentionally build the lives we want to share. The reason we put Person before People is because flourishing relationships include authenticity, vulnerability, and clear boundaries. We have to be OK with ourselves before we can fully embrace the fullness of others.

With a basic understanding of the idea of Circles of Connection, I want to talk about each circle and the type of emotional and practical support we give and receive within them.

EMOTIONAL SUPPORT

Emotional support is about trust, intimacy, authenticity, and transparency. The people with whom we give and receive emotional support are usually people with whom we share similar values and perspectives. We also expect more from one another and offer more to one another. There may be, in this emotional support, some connection with our practical lives, our financial lives. But it's important to know that having people to talk to who will maintain our confidentiality as well as tell us the truth is very valuable. People can be with us in life without doing physical labor or transferring currency.

Within our emotionally supportive circle of People, it's important to have one or more individuals we call Thought Partners. These are the people that help us process life at the deeper emotional, spiritual, and mindful levels, where we are deciding who we are and how we want to be in the world. They challenge our views and the decisions we make on our life path, even our Life Compass Plans. They're usually the people that are able to view us through a non-judgmental lens and are more able to nurture us and help us gain needed insights. We feel a sense of energy and encouragement when we're with them. I hope you have at least one Thought Partner. I have benefited greatly from a few Thought Partners throughout my life including a spiritual director, life coach, and therapist. I have also had mentors, close friends, and sponsors in this role. I mention them here because they used some questions, ways of checking in, and listening skills that enriched my life in significant ways. Give yourself the gift of having Thought Partners and making time with them a priority.

All the people who give us emotional support are precious. They're part of what makes human life worth living. Romantic love can be part of this, but this is more than what we have with our life partners or spouses. I've experienced emotional support through my Circles of Connection, from close friends, relatives, colleagues, even a barista friend who takes breaks when I arrive for a cup of java. Think about who these particular people are in your life and the variety of ways they emotionally support you and you emotionally support them. These are relationships to be nurtured and savored.

It's important to note that emotional support can flow in either one or two directions. When it flows in one direction, it basically means we provide support without the expectation of receiving it in return. We experience this with our young children, with some of the people we have as friends, and, at times, with the people we've chosen to invest our lives in. We can be on the receiving end of this as well. It is OK for someone to support us emotionally and all we can give back is gratitude.

Being aware of our relationships that require "one-way" emotional support can help us better manage our energy levels when we're engaged in them. Have you ever heard yourself or someone else say, "(So and so) is wearing me out"? That's literally what's happening. When there's not a mutual exchange of emotional energy, it's easy to experience exhaustion. It's perfectly natural to have this dynamic in some of our relationships. For example, a friend of mine recently said, "George, my mom is driving me crazy. Every time I call her, she immediately goes into telling me every detail of her day and every ache and pain she's experiencing. I never get a word in edgewise. I used to call her, and she'd ask me how *I'm* doing, but not anymore." This often happens with parents and kids as we age. Yes, my friend is frustrated, but she's also grieving the loss of the "one-way" emotional support her mother gave her as a kid and the "two-way" emotional support she's experienced over the years in her adult-to-adult relationship with her mother. At this point in life, her mother is simply not capable of giving the same emotional support she once gave. Chances are, my friend's mother experienced the same dynamic with her mother.

The same can be said of friendships. I've met people in my journey of recovery who have helped me without my ability to support them much at all in life. And I've met people in recovery who chose to sit down with me and unpack their lives. They have, over the course of time, become close friends and even models of how to live life.

One key to maintaining our health and well-being is to be mindful of "one-way" and "two-way" emotional support and to surround ourselves with people who can provide the support *we need* in order to replenish our energy. When we're energized, we can do a much better job giving "one-way" support to those we love who need it. It's a cycle of give-and-take, balance, and boundaries. Awareness is the key to mastery in this area.

PRACTICAL SUPPORT

Practical support involves trust, expectations, and the cost of time and money. It's more matter-of-fact and provided by people who deliver a service, paid or unpaid. It also may or may not include emotional support or personal interactions. Practical support can also flow one way or both ways. When we depend on people in practical ways — for finances, for sharing the chores around the house, for taking care of the things that need to be taken care of in life — we share practical support. And that practical support involves a different kind of vulnerability. Family members, friends and neighbors sometimes provide this kind of support without having emotional intimacy. That's why I believe it's helpful to separate the two. Getting clear on who will provide our emotional support and who will provide our practical support helps keep expectations in harmony with the roles we define in our Essential Conversations.

COMPASSION AND EMPATHY

In terms of emotional and practical support, I feel it's worth noting the difference between compassion and empathy. Understanding this difference can make *all the difference* in the way we experience our relationships. Let me explain.

Compassion means to feel *for* the pain and struggles of someone. While there are people who lack compassion, it's common for most of us to feel for and, at times, even practically help others who are suffering. We may not have experienced what they're suffering, per se, but we can imagine what it would be like to experience it. Empathy means to feel *with* someone. When we empathize with someone, we are reliving a similar experience or form of suffering that we've known at some point in our life.

Knowing the difference between the two helps us in three primary ways.

First, it guides how we communicate with those who are suffering. For example, years ago, a close friend of ours shared the news that she had a miscarriage. She and her husband had longed for a baby. They had spent a few years and a great deal of money on the best medical support available. All of us who were their friends hoped and prayed and rejoiced when she let us know she was pregnant. Now we were supporting them through this huge loss. Tammy and I had two children at the time and did not have difficulties having them. I entered the pain of learning the difference between compassion and empathy with the well-meaning words, "I know you're disappointed, but you can try again." I am hurting now remembering those words. I would have helped more with silence. I had compassion but not empathy. Tammy's face said it all as my words landed on our friend's ears and hearts. I had enough sense to stop talking and let her guide the conversation as it moved forward. She could listen with the empathy of one who had felt the kicks and all the changes of being pregnant. They wept together, and I left them alone to share something I could not. Another friend who had had a miscarriage could empathize on an even deeper level than Tammy, simply because of her own journey.

Secondly, understanding the difference between compassion and empathy helps us do an emotional "check in" with ourselves. I've learned the hard way that it's sometimes challenging to emotionally separate from the people we have empathy with. When we have empathy with someone, we feel their pain because it was once our pain. We're able to identify with them so deeply that, even with the best intentions, we can end up losing the capacity to stand outside the struggle. This can result in harm to both parties. We will lose ourselves if we try to "save" someone else. We will also steal the life lessons that were intended for that person to learn on *their* journey. For example, a friend of mine, I'll call her Gina, spent a significant amount of time, money, and emotional energy attempting to help a friend of hers move figuratively and literally out of an abusive relationship. Gina understood on a deep level the pain and fear that a person faces in this situation. Unfortunately, her friend wasn't ready to face that pain and fear, and chose to remain with the abuser for years. As a result, every time the abuse escalated, she would call Gina. With every call, Gina was sure that *this* would be the time her friend would make the move, which prompted Gina to sacrifice her time, sometimes money, and emotions again. The abusive cycle had made its way into the friendship, and Gina was angry and exhausted. Although there was a risk she would lose the friendship, Gina realized she needed to first care for herself by distancing from her friend. She did this by sharing her feelings of anger and resentment and setting strong boundaries. Understandably, her friend initially felt rejected but over time realized that the pain of potentially losing her friendship with Gina (and others) was more than the pain she would experience leaving her abuser. This "tough love" was part of what needed to happen in order for her to make the move. It was also what Gina needed in order to honor herself, staying true to her Person.

Thirdly, it helps us determine where we spend our energy, time, and money. As we think through our Circles of Connection and our Life

Compass Plan, we'll intentionally determine who we'll reorder our lives for so that we can help reduce their suffering. For example, I loved learning through my friend April about two siblings (Quinn and Nikki), who intentionally combined three households to reduce the suffering and secure the future of their aging parents. This was a drastic change for all of them, but they made it through and now are beyond happy to be living in three separate spaces within one house. It took a lot of planning and creativity, but they now have a multigenerational home that is mortgage-free. Quinn, his wife, Vickie, and their three girls live on the main floor; Nikki and her partner, Chris, live in a small apartment on the side of the house: and Quinn and Nikki's parents live in a two-bedroom apartment in the basement. They are living in alignment with their Life Compass Plan that was driven by their compassion for their parents and one another.

The reordering of our lives doesn't have to be as drastic as combining households. We can make small changes here and there that help reduce the suffering of others. For example, there may be certain humanitarian causes we decide to financially contribute to that involve people on the outer periphery of our Circles, people we'll never actually meet. Or, we may decide to volunteer our time to help mentor someone who's walking through something we've walked through, such as domestic violence or addiction or widowhood, etc. The point is, compassion and empathy empower us to support our people and motivates them to support us. Knowing the difference between the two enables us to pay attention to why and how we choose to show up for others and why and how they choose to show up for us.

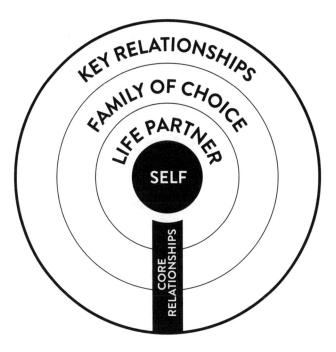

CORE RELATIONSHIPS

Our Core Relationships are the People at the center of our Circles of Connection. They are the people we depend on most for emotional and practical support, and they depend on us. In some cases, we'll change their diapers if they need us to, and they'll do the same for us. They may be family, our life partner or spouse, or our closest friends. These are the people we call at 3 a.m., drop off at the car dealership on our way to work, or meet in the Emergency Room. Many of them enrich our daily lives and, with all of them, we help one another through the tough times. It's a give-and-take relationship that involves direct care and emotional presence that we don't share with others. Quinn and Nikki's story above is a great example of this, but keep in mind our Core Relationships don't have to necessarily include our family of origin or relatives.

As we move through the stages of life, some of the People in our Core Relationships will leave and others will remain. Some of the people I've met along my journey were people I considered part of my Core Relationships at a particular time. We had close friends who had children the same age as ours and they were an important part of our lives as we raised the children and made memories. We treasure those times, but we do not share life as we did. Others have remained part of my Core Relationships — 20, 30, even 40-plus years later. Our Core Relationships play a significant part in our Life Compass Plan, so it's important for us to think about who these people are now and how we'll include them in our future. For example, one of my Core Relationships is a close friend who's been with me since 1972 and will remain in my Core Relationships circle for life. We've had a variety of conversations about how each of us can honor the other in this Life Stage and the ones to come. Of course, we don't know exactly what the future holds for either one of us but we do know we'll be each other's advocate. The Essential Conversations we've had about life and death and the stages in between have strengthened our friendship beyond what either of us could have ever imagined. If he dies unexpectedly, I'll be there for his family and vice versa. These are the types of bonds that secure us today and in the future.

A quick side note here: Advocacy is a very important part of our Core Relationships. We've all had advocates as part of the natural progression from birth to adulthood. Parents, caregivers, teachers, encouragers, mentors, and the people who stepped up for us shaped who we are and the lives we live. I see many who do not have the support systems and advocates I had growing up. We feel for those who lack advocates as children. Our world is not just, and some bear more of the burden of the injustices we have yet to address. I want us to remember and plan for the fact that when we become adults, we still need advocates. It may be a short-term illness or a crisis beyond our control that calls them into action, but we will need them.

We will talk specifically about the basic roles advocates play in Chapter 6 (Protection) but begin to consider now who in your Core Relationships you want to be your advocate when you need one. Who will be there for you? Sometimes, we will use professionals as advocates. An attorney is an obvious example. They are part of a Life Compass Plan. But, if you can't make decisions, care for yourself, or simply need some help getting through a tough time, "Who ya gonna call?" Unless you are in a current crisis, let the Life Compass Plan protocol help you choose your advocates as part of the process. You don't want to avoid choosing and empowering people to help you. You also don't want to trust people who are not able to do what you need done in a pinch.

SELF

The center circle in our Circles of Connection is the self. It's you, it's me, it's the Person. The first thing we must do as we build our Core Relationships is define ourselves: who we are, what we value, and how we will find significance. As previously mentioned, here is where it becomes important to take ownership of being the Author of our Life Story. First we develop our character and then we choose the characters who will make up our Circles of Connections. It's through our characters, our People, that we build and leave our legacy.

LIFE PARTNER

The second circle out is a circle not everyone has, but is one that many people seek, and that is to have a life partner, a spouse, a Person who enters our lives with the commitment to stay through the rest of the journey. In his book *Getting the Love You Want*, Harville Hendrix introduces an idea that I have found very helpful. He states that we all need at least one relationship where there are no exits. There's one thing I'd like to be clear on — he's not suggesting we stay in an abusive relationship or one where we can't express ourselves or feel trapped. Instead, Hendrix is talking about a place we choose to stay with another so that we can be secure not only in what's happening today, but in whatever might happen as time moves forward.

As I read Hendrix's work, I remembered a day when my wife and I were having a disagreement and it became one of the worst days of our relationship, and yet a lesson that has continued to teach me greatly. Right now, I can't even remember what the disagreement was about, but it was early in our marriage, and it was intense. At least, I was experiencing it as very intense. I was raised in a household where things could become violent when tensions got high, and I had made a choice not to ever be violent in my relationships. So, I was needing some space. I was going to have to leave our apartment for a time, but I had every intention of re-engaging with her when I was calm and able to process whatever it was we were disagreeing about.

In order to reassure her, I said my now infamous statement that my friends to this day joke about at parties. I said to her, "You don't have to worry. We're going to work through this. **You're my only option.**" Yes. That was one of those moments that's funny now but not so funny at the time. What I meant was that I was in it for the long haul. I wasn't going anywhere. I was not going to trade her in for someone else. I would stay. I would work through things. What she heard was that I was stuck, and that I didn't have any other option than to be married to her.

Hendrix eloquently unpacks the concept of choice: While we want to have relationships where there are no exits, the quality, and the beauty, and the capacity to mature and grow in those relationships actually exists by *continuously choosing* to be in them. Whereas I'm a proponent of marriage, the institution itself doesn't secure our futures or guarantee a relationship "without exits." Married or not, a healthy relationship is based on choice.

There are many folks I've met who have lived through the excruciating pain of a divorce and have decided they'll never marry again but have chosen to have a life partner. The choice not to marry is a Life Compass choice I respect. Marriage is a legal entity that carries certain benefits and protections. When couples choose to not have those benefits and protections, securing the relationship from a financial and other administrative standpoint can get more complicated. This is where Life Compass Planning and Essential Conversations can be incredibly helpful. For example, Jim has been divorced twice and has three kids — one from his first marriage and two from his second. He's in a relationship with Susan, who is also divorced and has two kids from her only marriage. Jim and Susan have been together for five years and are continuously choosing to be in a relationship with no exits but have decided they don't want to marry. As Jim and Susan build their Life Compass as a couple, they will make decisions about how they will invest their energy, time, and money — not only in one another but also in the children they both brought to their relationship, and perhaps even in their former spouses and the in-laws they formed relationships with when they were married. In their Essential Conversations, they'll talk about who they want involved in their care in the event one of them becomes ill (for example, Susan and her ex-husband, Frank, are good friends, and Susan would want Jim to invite Frank in to help care for her, if needed) and put the documentation in place that will ensure they both have access to one another in the event of an unplanned hospitalization. They'll also determine how their individual and combined money will pass when one of them dies (Jim has a niece on his ex-wife's side who's like a daughter to him. He wants to ensure she receives a percentage of his money if there's any left after Susan dies).

We'll further discuss how to protect our Core Relationships, including our spouses and life partners, later in the book. You may or may not have someone in that role at this moment ... or ever, which is fine. There are many single people who are flourishing in their lives with Core

Relationships. Being single doesn't mean you are alone in life. I see many people flourish with their family of origin and/or their Family of Choice, which happens to be the next circle.

FAMILY OF CHOICE

The third circle in our Circles of Connection is what I call the Family of Choice. This is not equal to our relatives who live nearby. That still exists in a few places, but most of us depend on people who are not related to us by blood or marriage. A word coming into our vocabulary is "framily," the good friends who become part of the family we choose for ourselves. I am fully committed to people who are framily. The lives of these people and their children's lives matter to me. We depend on each other like family. I have relatives who are part of my Family of Choice and relatives who aren't part of my Family of Choice. This is one of the gifts and responsibilities of *adulting* in our world — we get to choose our family members.

We are responsible *to*, and responsible *for* one another in our Family of Choice, and it's important to know who those people are now, and who they will be in the future. Our Family of Choice may have people who enter and exit later in life. Children grow up, people move, people die, relationships change and, for many other reasons, our Family of Choice will have exits.

One place where this is obvious is in your household. The people who have lived with Tammy and me in our home have changed many times over the years. This is not unusual. Our sons came home from the hospital at their birth and headed off into their adult adventures later. We have had relatives and friends spend some extended time with us in transitions. We have had our children and our parents in and out of our household. It was part of being family in the Life Stories we shared. The experience of sharing life and living space had challenges, benefits and many joys. It may sound strange but some people who are in our household will not become part of your Family of Choice. The way you share those days is part of a plan but does not come with all the promises and long-term plans shared in a Family of Choice.

The people who are part of our household for a time can be wonderful parts of our Life Story and still not become Family of Choice. We made friends with Victor while he was in our city working on a contract with a local company. He lived by himself in a short-term rental property and planned to return to Europe, where he lived, in a few months. He became ill and moved into our home while he healed and then stayed until his contract ended. He will always be a friend, and we came to know and care about his family while he lived with us. We do not communicate often now. We will always be grateful for the great memories we made and his contributions to our home and Life Stories. He paid rent. He did chores. He taught us how life was where he lived. For a few months, we shared life and were all better off. Some of those in our Family of Choice met him, but our Life Compasses are guiding us into other places.

It's good to remember we can move people closer to the center, and move people farther out into the wider concentric circles, based on the factors that matter to us and support our Life Compasses. It's also good to introduce our relatives to those Family of Choice members who are not relatives. Often, we do life with our Family of Choice and when an accident or sudden illness occurs, our relatives outside of our Family of Choice enter the picture without knowing the non-relatives we consider to be equally part of our family. When this happens, it's easy for those Family of Choice members to be dismissed simply because many people operate from the "blood is thicker than water" mindset. This can be a tremendous loss for us and our Family of Choice members. I've known people who have been the best of friends, relating as a Family of Choice for years and, yet, didn't have a chance to say goodbye because the relatives who showed up at the end of life didn't have their contact information, or worse yet, didn't view the relationship as a priority because the person "wasn't family."

Your Family of Choice doesn't have to meet your biological/by marriage family in person. You can simply talk to them all to let them know how important these people are to you, and ensure everyone has each other's contact information.

KEY RELATIONSHIPS

The People who make up the fourth circle in our Core Relationships are our Key Relationships. You might prefer the words vital relationships. These relationships tend to have more fluidity. In other words, our Key Relationships have people journeying into and out of that circle as each stage of life unfolds, but they are vital. They are important to us. They provide stability and safety. They enrich our lives. They are people we reference in our everyday life, and yet there are ways in which we're responsible to them that are different than our Family of Choice.

Key Relationships include the people I like to call our *Joy Camp*. We often refer to the people in our Joy Camp as our friends. Some we work with, some we share hobbies with, others we've met through friends of friends. They're not essential in the ways that a life partner or Family of Choice would be, and their presence is more fluid, but they're there and they're very important.

My father was a man who did not form a lot of intimate relationships in his life, but he had a huge Joy Camp. He had a whole lot of friends. He felt close to his friends, and his friends felt close to him. Along the way, some of them stepped up in ways that seemed to move them closer to the Family of Choice circle. They became the ones who showed up in the difficult times, and stood with my father and helped him as he faced his challenges with dementia and the end of life. I watched as they did what they needed to and proved they were Joy Camp and so much more. They continued to share stories with him and he with them. They told stories of their time in war together. They told stories of growing up in the same era, having the same memories. And so, when it comes to the concentric circle of Key Relationships, I wish for you to define those relationships as you choose. Let people be important to you, and allow yourself to be important to them. They may not be a Family of Choice, but they are very important in our lives nonetheless.

OUTER CONNECTIONS

With the first circle being Self; second, our Life Partner or Spouse; the third, our Family of Choice; the fourth, our Key Relationships, we then move into the boundless outer sphere that we call the Outer Connections — our social, secondary, and tertiary relationships. They're not unimportant but they do not include as big of a commitment to emotional and practical support as our Core Relationships. These people may be colleagues, teachers, coaches, casual friends, people who are in our lives for a time, and/or people we've shared an event in life with and feel very connected to because of the memory of that event. Their relationship is mostly a matter of the circumstance, season of life, or the occasion. Some of these Outer Connections are more transactional in nature — for example, people who have hired us or we've hired to do contract work and/or people we may support across the globe.

I know when my dad was going through the end of life, I hired some in-home health care workers, and they bonded with my dad and me. They did not feel like contract workers after providing such compassionate help and sharing their own stories from their lives and family. They weren't relatives or Family of Choice and yet, when my dad's memorial service came, they were there, and their presence added to the richness of that gathering, and to the story of my dad's life and death. Since his death, we've shared a couple of phone calls and have affection in our hearts for one another. We have memories of working through some very difficult times with my father. They'll always matter in terms of the memories I have, and the value they were to my and my dad's lives, but they have not remained Key Relationships.

Just because they're in the Outer Connections, don't dismiss the impact these people can have on our lives. Take teachers, for example. In the book *The Village Effect*, Susan Pinker points to a research study that included 2.5 million American children. The outcomes revealed that students who were taught by a great (rather than average) teacher for just one year were more likely to go to college, more likely to go to an excellent college, were less likely to be teenage mothers, and earned more as adults — an average of $250,000 more over a lifetime. As adults, they also lived in nicer neighborhoods and were more likely to save for their retirement.

My wife is an elementary school teacher, and over the years I've been in public when she was greeted by former students, and I watched their faces. I heard the tenderness and affection in their voices as they expressed appreciation for the work my wife had done as their teacher. She particularly loves kindergartners. It's her favorite age, and she's really good when those children are learning the joy and the curiosities of reading, discovering life, and creating, experiencing, and sharing stories. We were checking out at Fresh Market recently and the cashier looked at Tammy with a sheepish smile. "Hello Mrs. Fuller. This is Justin." Tammy's face lit up and the couple in line behind us signaled that there was no hurry as he started telling her how much she meant to him and how he was starting graduate school in the fall. He asked for a hug and we floated home. The Outer Connections can be precious.

Our Circles of Connection are what make up our community. Julianne Holt-Lunstad, who's at Brigham Young University, has done a lot of research on the benefits of relationships, and she says the two things we need are close relationships and social integration. Close relationships are the Core Relationships that we've been talking about. Social integration is about how we interact with people as we go through our day. She describes people living in a community where they're catching up with one another, and telling stories of neighbors and family as they pass on the streets or stand in line at the store.

People who are old enough may remember communities that had this as part of everyday life. In today's reality, finding a community like this is still possible but it takes a little more work, especially in our larger cities. The hope in Life Compass Living is to intentionally build these types of communities back into our lives. We need close relationships and social integration to flourish.

I have a friend, Taylor, whose business helps create community in the ways we need. He owns what used to be a country store called Taylor's Store. Taylor is a people person. Honestly, I've never met anyone who genuinely loves every kind of person as much as he does. He has his own views that we enjoy discussing but he learned through his own journey of hardships to not be critical of how people are, even though he will confront rudeness as part of the culture he has built at Taylor's Store. The city grew, and his store is now near an interstate highway and is very busy. It's now not only a place to buy gas and a snack, it's where you see familiar faces, share stories, and make friends with people you would have no other reason to know. I am called "Pastor George" there, though I am not a minister to any of the regulars that come through. His son, Ben, has taken on leadership as of late and has continued the legacy his dad built with the store. His daughter, Melissa, helps with the digital life of the store from her house in Florida. Spending time there is truly a magical experience. I get fair trade coffee, local beers, wine after meeting the winemakers, and even the fish bait needed when taking my grandchildren to the lake. I also play some music there twice a year, with friends mostly, so we can sing along to the oldies we like best. I cried when Tom, one of the regulars, died after his long battle with Parkinson's disease. A few of us circled up like we were at a sacred campfire to laugh and tell stories of his quirks, compassion, and the ability to always have a cigar in his hand and never light it.

Taylor is in my Key Relationships Circle, a Thought Partner and friend, and the rest of the folks there are in my Outer Circles. They all matter to me and help me believe we have the potential to share life with compassion across the divides of our culture better than others who don't have a place like Taylor's Store. As we develop our Life Compass Plan, we must start at the center in our Circles of Connection, but I hope our society as a whole learns to invest more in the Outer Circles, too. There's a sacredness there that our world needs.

I encourage you to begin thinking through your Circles of Connection. Make lists of your People and place them in the corresponding circles. My hope is that you will experience more gratitude for the people in your life, and begin to think and plan more intentionally about how you want to participate in their lives, and how they'll participate in yours.

TRAJECTORY OF READINESS: ACCEPTANCE, AWARENESS, ACTION

Now that we've started working on who we are as a Person and have identified our People within our Circles of Connection, it's time to "get real" about life. Building our capacity to accept life and be present and participate in it as it is — not how we want it to be or hoped it would be but exactly as it is — is a process that I call the "Trajectory of Readiness."

There's a framework that emerged from the 12-step community called the Three As of Change (Acceptance, Awareness, and Action). I've found this framework to be a particularly helpful tool that we can use on our Trajectory of Readiness.[7] This type of work is informed and unpacked in writing on emotional intelligence. We need skills that keep us from being controlled by emotions and able to fully utilize our intelligence guided by our own self-determination.[8] Right now, you may be experiencing so much anxiety that you simply can't be open, willing, or able to accept what's actually happening in your life. And that's perfectly OK. Coming to accept life on life's terms takes time and work in our mindfulness practices. We each have our own experience of life, and it takes time to adjust our ability to talk about and accept what's actually occurring in the days that we share. The Trajectory of Readiness is similar to the stages of grief. Grieving has common elements, but we each have our own time frames when it comes to accepting a loss and adjusting ourselves to the new reality that's taking shape. It often begins with a statement like, "I can't believe it." or "I don't know what to do without ____." Being aware that we all land at different places on our Trajectory of Readiness can help us be more patient with one another as we work on sharing life.

In the cases where there is an urgent need to make decisions and take action, this can help us offer compassion to those who have not fully accepted all the implications of what is unfolding before them. Many times — in a state of emergency — we're not necessarily aware of the things that matter. For example, a woman, I'll call her, Sandi, lost her husband, Matt, to death by suicide. She was walking around Kohl's doing some last-minute shopping for a school field trip scheduled the next day when she received a call from an unknown number. Most of the time, she didn't answer such calls but, for some reason, this particular day she did. The call was from a police officer who told her that a neighbor had found Matt dead on their back porch. Needless to say, Sandi went immediately into a state of shock and disbelief. She somehow drove to their home and met the police officer, but she can't remember to this day making that drive nor the majority of the details of what occurred for weeks after the incident. Having lived through a number of sudden deaths themselves, Sandi's sister-in-law and brother immediately sprang into action. Her sister-in-law notified Matt's employer of his death and got the ball rolling on administrative processes that needed to happen there, made funeral arrangements, and wrote the obituary. Sandi's brother, a former police officer, made sure the porch where Matt's death occurred was cleaned up and then contacted her landlord to ensure she could get out of her lease. Thankfully, Sandi's sister-in-law and brother were at a different place on their Trajectory of Readiness. Their life experiences had equipped them to better understand the most important action steps to take following an unexpected death.

Two years later, Sandi is at a different place on her Trajectory of Readiness. She's been able to help friends who have since lived through a similar experience and has even made sure her end-of-life wishes are known to her sons. She doesn't plan to die anytime soon but, having lived through this experience, she now understands the critical need to ensure there is a plan in place that will make her passing less stressful as for her kids, extended family, and friends.

While writing this section, I was reflecting on the time when my wife, Tammy, was diagnosed with cancer, and I had my own Trajectory of Readiness journey to fully embrace life on life's terms. Early on, I didn't want to accept the fact that she had advanced cancer. I was not aware of the full diagnosis, nor of the treatment plan, nor of the prognosis beyond the treatment plan ... and I didn't want to be an active participant. I was incredibly anxious. It was very hard for me to relate to people, and to life, during the days where we were going through surgery, and biopsies, and meetings with doctors, and discussing treatment plans. But, over the course of several weeks, I made progress, we made progress.

It was also a Trajectory of Readiness process for my kids, our Family of Choice and our Key Relationships. We were all grieving Tammy's healthy life that was in the past (thankfully, just for that moment in time). We slowly entered into *acceptance* as we waited for the biopsy and its interpretation. We then moved into *awareness* as we learned about the treatment options. And, finally, we stepped into *action* with surgeries, chemotherapy, and radiation.

The Trajectory of Readiness is part of how our minds, our selves, our souls, and our way of thinking have to be allowed to move. As the days and weeks and months went by, I talked about it more, and spent time in my own private space where I was able to reflect, and journal, and pray. It was then that I was able to make progress in accepting the reality that was now part of Tammy's and my life. We went through the process again and again as we learned about what we were dealing with, how we could treat it, and what the long-term prognosis was beyond treatment. I love remembering how we seemed to be ready for each day, even though there was a lot to process and we often needed to cry and talk and sit in the silence where mortals find the capacity to live life even when it's messy and tenuous. This is just one illustration of the many happenings in life that invite us to be patient with ourselves and with one another. Being ready did not mean doing everything "right" or being "happy" all the time. It meant being in this readiness trajectory together.

Tammy and I got a double recliner where we sat, slept, prayed, and suffered together. When it was all over, we sold that recliner and yet we aspire to always sit, sleep, pray and suffer through whatever is ahead in our shared life.

Where are you on your Trajectory of Readiness? This is a challenging question that can trigger significant anxiety in all of us. Who knows what life will bring our way or when. **My goal through the Life Compass protocol is to help us become aware that none of us will live forever and we will all need and will be needed at some point in our lives. This reality is a sacred part of being human. The more we accept this about ourselves and one another, the more aware we become. Through our Essential Conversations, this awareness will empower us with a "readiness" to face whatever may come our way together.** Let's start investing in our relationships now so that we can better celebrate our sunny days and walk more elegantly through our rainy ones.

By living in alignment with our Life Compass and the Life Compass of those we love, we have the amazing opportunity to celebrate in all of life's occasions — the joyous seasons and the painful seasons. Our "togetherness" allows us to discover joy even in the midst of pain. There are three words that have emerged from my experiences caring for my parents, in-laws, and wife and from sitting beside countless others in similar situations: Facts. Power. Ability. These words guide my own Trajectory of Readiness in any given scenario and I use them when working with others as they face the unforeseen events life brings their way.

FACTS, POWER, ABILITY

The first thing we must do as we begin our journey together to better understand and accept life is come to some common understanding of the Facts. Often, our brains need help sorting out the Facts from all the emotion and interpretation that clouds our understanding. I would record the doctor's appointments through various illnesses with Tammy and other people in my life. On many occasions, I was really glad I had the recordings. While I thought I heard the doctor correctly, and while I thought I remembered what the doctor said correctly, the recording proved otherwise. So, the first word is Facts.

The second is the word Power. This is about who actually has the Power to make decisions and determine what happens next. We often spend time on decisions that are not ours and miss the places where we do have Power or influence.

For example, I was sitting with three siblings, two daughters and a son, and we were beginning to discuss the crisis their mother was in. She had dementia and was no longer able to make decisions determining her own life. That was clear to everyone; it was a Fact. Before we formally began our meeting, the two sisters talked about what they thought was best for mom, where she should be, how she should be cared for, and what decisions needed to be made. During this time, I noticed that their brother was sitting silently waiting for the meeting to begin. As I began the meeting, I first explained that we needed to establish the Facts related specifically to Power. I asked if there was a durable power of attorney and medical power of attorney in place. The brother said "yes" and that he was the one named in both. The durable power of attorney gave him the authority to make financial and property decisions for his mom while she is living. The medical power of attorney gave him the authority to make decisions directing her medical care. She also had a living will that expressed how she wished to be supported at the end of life. All three knew about the living will. Then I asked, "Does your mother have a will?" And the brother said, "Yes," and I said, "Who's the executor of her will?" And he said, "I am."

And so, I turned to the two sisters and I said, "We'll all be able to collect, and gather information about the Facts of what your mother needs, what resources are available now, and what she's going to need in the future. However, there's one thing that I want you to understand. Since your brother has been given the medical power of attorney and the durable power of attorney, he will be the one who ultimately has the authority to make the decisions that need to be made. So that means that, as we talk, we all have the ability to inform the decisions. We all have the ability to create the best future possible for your mother. We have the capacity to create the synergy, and even transform how things are happening now and will happen in the future." After an extended silence, I continued, "We have the ability to give your brother all that he needs to make the best decisions. But right now, because your mother can't change those legal documents, he has the Power to make the decisions."

The third word is Ability. The good news is that the brother quickly said, "I expect that my sisters will have a lot of wisdom. They know Mom well. They love Mom a lot. They see her regularly." It became a beautiful experience of three people who love their mother making decisions together. That's the Ability we have when we have a shared understanding of Facts, understand who has the Power, and use that Ability to support the people who have the Power as they make the decisions. This makes it possible to make decisions that move through transitions and growing needs with elegance.

This is true at every stage of life and in all the ways we support one another. Minor children, family members, friends, and co-workers all ask us to enter into decision-making with them. When we have some degree of common understanding of the FACTS, POWER, and ABILITY present in those decisions, we increase our capacity to own our roles and make better decisions.

ESSENTIAL CONVERSATIONS: THE MOST IMPORTANT CONVERSATIONS YOU'LL EVER HAVE

As I mentioned in Chapter One, Life Compass Living is powered and directed by **Essential Conversations**, a communication guide developed along with my friend and colleague Dr. Amy D'Aprix. In a nutshell, Essential Conversations are about **talking to the most important people about the most important things in our lives**. I am grateful to Amy for how she has enriched the lives of so many with her work. I'm also grateful that she's agreed to embed her Essential Conversations material within the Life Compass protocol. She says, "Everyone deserves an Essential Conversation," and I couldn't agree more.

I discovered Amy and her framework when I attended a training she facilitated as part of what was called the Essential Conversations Project. The framework was designed for professionals such as therapists, mediators, coaches, etc. to help families better communicate and plan for the later stages in life, when care is most often needed. Amy's goal in creating her Essential Conversations framework was to get families talking *before* a crisis happens. We both agree that, too often, family relationships are heavily strained — sometimes completely torn — in the midst of a Life Quake (a life transition that happens without warning and/or without a plan). It's common for adult children and their parents to avoid conversations that include *anything* related to someone having a potential illness, such as cancer or falling and breaking a hip or having a heart attack or stroke or, worse yet, dying. But this is what happens in life. This is exactly what the Trajectory of Readiness is all about. Where will Mom go after her hospitalization? She can't live at home but can't afford assisted living or in-home care. Will Susie take her into her home? She's the daughter and lives closest. Oh, wait. Mom can't go there. Susie travels extensively for her job and has a husband and three kids. What if she goes to Tom's house? He's single, lives only two hours away, and, as we all know, is her *favorite* anyway. Tom: "Uh, guys, no, way. I'm trying to get my new business started plus I have a lot of steps in my house. *I* can't take her in."

Let's say in this scenario that Susie rearranges her life and home to accommodate her mother. At first, it seems like it'll be a great experience. Her husband and kids will have this idyllic bonding with her mom. Just like an AARP commercial. Her kids will play in the backyard while her mom swings and her husband grills the steaks. She'll make their salad and smile to herself as she watches them through the kitchen window. Sounds amazing, right? Well, not quite. In reality, Mom is much slower than she used to be and doesn't feel like leaving her bedroom, much less going outside and sitting in a swing. Plus, she's depressed that she can't live in her house any longer. As a matter of fact, she's snappy too and demanding of everyone in the house.

Susie had no idea how disruptive this would be on her marriage, their bank account or the impact it would have on her kids. Over time, she finds herself resentful of her mom for not saving enough for her long-term care, resentful that she's having to miss so many days of work, and furious with her brother — with whom she used to have a great relationship — for not stepping up more. She feels even more furious and distraught when her mom eventually dies and she learns that she has to split the little money her mom had left with not only her brother but also one of her mom's siblings, who's 83 years old and in a nursing home. Susie: "What the hell? I'm the one who has spent the last three years of my life running Mom to doctor appointments, cooking her meals, getting her groceries, taking her for haircuts, helping her with showers, paying her bills ... basically managing her entire life, and I have to equally split what's left of her money with *TOM AND UNCLE JOHN*? Really? You've got to be kidding me! Don't get me wrong, I love Mom, but this has been the hardest job I've ever had!"

This exact scenario and countless others like it are the reasons Amy created her Essential Conversations process and we integrated elements of it into the Life Compass protocol. I feel deep sadness when I meet folks who have aging parents who live alone and have no idea what they will do when the crisis inevitably knocks on their door. I feel even more sad for folks who would like to have a conversation but their parents won't talk about "it." The good news is that we can work around those who aren't willing or able to participate with something I call *parallel planning*, which we'll dive into more below.

While Amy's framework was initially targeted at families in mid-life and beyond, these conversations are essential and incredibly beneficial in every stage of life. Making the choice to marry. Preparing for babies. Getting our kids prepared for college. Making a career change. Losing a job. Buying a new house. Relocating to a new city. Moving through divorce. You name it. Essential Conversations are a vital part of helping any and all life transitions be less stressful and, for some, more joyful.

Before I go through the specific progression about how to have Essential Conversations, I want to offer a couple of skills I believe are worth understanding and developing.

THE STARTING PLACE IS NOW

The first one is to remember that the ***starting place is now***. Start with the relationships we have now. Start with the level of self-awareness we have now. Start with the willingness for authenticity and transparency we have now. And start with the boundaries we have now. All we have is now. We can't wait for us to be in the "right" space or time or we'll miss the opportunity in front of us.

In the openness created as we remember that the starting place is now, we become better able to begin our Essential Conversations without judgment, without condemnation. We can talk without preloading our reactions, or anticipating that everyone will deal with things the way they've always dealt with things. Reactions, judgment, and condemnation produce isolation, and that's the opposite direction that we want to go in having our Essential Conversations. With "now" as the starting place, we're able to release the expectations that may hamper our ability to really be present with one another and experience authenticity. We are all somewhere in the Trajectory of Readiness, and we cannot be anywhere else for now.

THE POWER OF LERA!

The second skill is a collection of wisdom built by Dr. Amy. In her work with financial advisors and other professionals seeking a way to establish stronger relationships with their clients, she teaches a conversational style built on the acronym LERA. I'm going to describe it in just a few words, but I hope that you'll recognize that these words invite deeper reflection and an opportunity to grow and improve the way we communicate.

The L is for listening. There are many classes on how to listen well. Active listening was a class I took in grad school that has produced fruit in my life in so many ways. The ability to listen is huge in Essential Conversations. So, as you learn to actively listen, you'll learn to pay atten-tion to your breath and arrive in the moment. This skill opens us up to the reality being communicated by others. There are a variety of different books and online courses you can access to help you learn to actively listen. A couple that have been incredibly helpful to me are *Non-violent Communication* by Marshall Rosenberg and *Crucial Conversations: Tools for Talking When Stakes Are High* by Kerry Patterson, Joseph Grenny, Ron McMillan and Al Switzler.

E is to empathize. If you remember, I earlier made a distinction between compassion and empathy. One way that we can bring our best to Essential Conversations is to look for and give the gift of compassion and empathy to the people we're talking with. Oftentimes, especially in our Core Relationships, we will find that we have a lot in common. Even if the people and events we have in common were experienced very differently by each of us, we can look to empathize, to care, to offer compassion as we listen and as we bring our best to our Essential Conversations. It is like a saying I have heard all my life, "People need to know we care before they will care about what we know." You don't have to come up with a Hallmark line to effectively communicate empathy. Just saying something like "Wow, that sounds overwhelming" or "I'm sure that's scary" goes a long way in reassuring a person that you are present and listening.

R is for reframing. As we listen and empathize, we are then better able to be open to all we can learn as the conversations progress. We become better informed, honor everyone's experience and hopes, and are better equipped to compassionately reframe our lives, our relationships, and the decisions we are making together. I have seen people move from being adversaries to allies in my work as a mediator by simply bringing these skills into the conversations. As we reframe our understanding of the people and the issues, we can create a different future. Building on the example above, an illustration of reframing would be something like, "It may be scary, but the fact that you're talking about this is so courageous — and I can't tell you what a gift it is to me." Arriving in a compassionate space, to learn from one another and shape a shared future, is hard work. Don't miss the help in Brene Brown's book *Braving the Wilderness*.

A is for act. Many people begin Essential Conversations with outcomes in mind. Unless there is real urgency because of a crisis that cannot wait to be addressed, please honor the order of LERA in your Essential Conversations. Act is not last because it is the least important. It is actually the purpose of all that proceeds it. We want to act, in relationship to one another, in ways that come from our best selves, fully honoring one another's Life Compass and Life Story. That takes time and will be helped by these skills we are highlighting, along with any others that equip you to better share life. I would like to suggest that you build the capacity as best you can — beyond the urgency that may be present — to put acting (in other words, following-through) as something that happens later in the process than you might want as you begin.

Here's an example. Dawn was the primary caregiver for her uncle. In addition to caring for him, she worked a full-time job, so she didn't have a lot of spare time. Following the sudden passing of her aunt, she knew she needed to help her uncle update his will. Making the updates would require coordination with the attorney, plus she'd have to either drive him to the bank or arrange for a notary to visit his assisted living apartment. Again, more time she didn't necessarily have to spare. Since her uncle wasn't in a crisis, she was able to actually allow the process to occur over a two- to three-month period. She sat down and explained what needed to happen and actively listened to him. During their conversation, she was able to have compassion for how difficult it was to lose his wife and to be living alone after being married for over 40 years. Again, actively listening and empathizing. She then was able to reframe this activity as him ensuring that everything they had worked so hard for during their lifetime together would be handled in the way he wanted it to be. This gave him a sense of control when he was feeling completely out of control in his life. A few weeks after the updates were made, Dawn arranged for a notary to meet her at his apartment to witness his signature. It ended up being a beautiful overall experience between the two of them, plus her uncle enjoyed meeting the notary, which made it even more special. Dawn was able to listen, empathize, reframe, and then finally act.

THE POWER AND PEACE OF PARALLEL PLANNING

The third practical skill that I'd like you to understand and develop is called *Parallel Planning*. I define Parallel Planning as *making plans for our own lives while we walk alongside others who can't or won't make plans with us or as we wish them to.* I've learned over the years that I can have my own agendas, in terms of conversations, relationships, and plans. These have a lot more to do with my own needs and insecurities than I like to admit. This is true for all of us. We all operate from the place of getting our own needs met. There is no need to judge or deny that starting place. In fact, we must include self-care in all we do or we'll suffer. And we cannot be available to support others without maintaining our own lives. I propose there is a way to put ourselves first while making it possible for us to remain available to those in our Core Relationships without unnecessary chaos and suffering for everyone involved. Let me illustrate:

I remember when Tammy and I were in the midst of "the sandwich generation," a generation of people, typically in their 30s or 40s, responsible for bringing up their own children and for the care of their aging parents. There were many factors going on, and I realized, with Tammy's help, that I had no right to demand that people have conversations **and** no right to expect that they would participate in plans we might "suggest." No matter how wise I thought those suggestions were, I needed to realize that each person deserved to be given the full dignity of determining their own Life Story and creating their own plans based on their own Life Compass without me insisting that their Life Story and Life Compass become centered on what I was hoping for or what I thought might be best for them.

That was a hard lesson to learn. In fact, it created what was another one of the hardest lessons in my marriage. I share it here because it's an essential lesson in learning how to have Essential Conversations, listening to one another's Life Story and Life Compass and use Parallel Planning. We had visited Abilene, Texas, and found my wife's parents in a very difficult situation. When we talked to them on the telephone, they always told us that everything was OK. However, when we arrived, we were shocked when we discovered the state of their health and living conditions. They needed help. Tammy's mom needed some medical support immediately. Her physician was unaware of how she was struggling but, fortunately, he and his staff were very responsive. We spent a couple of days talking to her physician about the diagnosis and treatment plan for more than one condition and put in-home health care in place. Her parents were appreciative, and we left to continue our vacation toward the Rocky Mountains in our pop-up camper, feeling good that we had helped them find and connect to resources. They had the support they needed from professionals, as well as some relatives and friends that volunteered to help once they were aware of the needs.

Then came the horrible moment where Tammy and I were having a conversation reflecting on it. I was beginning to tell her what I thought needed to be done, and she was resistant to my ideas. I then made the statement that, in some ways, I wish I had never made, but am also glad I did because it became one of the most crucial and insightful moments in my own journey of caregiving. I said, "I would not let my parents suffer the way you let your parents suffer." Bang. Bang. Bang. That's the sound of my head hitting the proverbial brick wall once I realized the "awful" that just came out of my mouth. When I talk about this in the seminars I teach, this is usually when people laugh because its stupidity is obvious. I can laugh now because of grace. But, believe me when I say there was no laughter at that moment. These 14 words were the cause of tremendous angst.

Fortunately, my wife was wise and responded with profound insight. She said, "George, you seem anxious. Whose life are you anxious about? Whose life are we talking about?"

And I answered, "It's your parents' life."

"That's right," she answered. "It's not your life we're talking about. If you're worried about how their needs will impact our lives, then I suggest we make the decisions we want to make, do what we're willing to do, and say no when we want to say no. But, they want to live their life in Abilene and they have every right to live their life there as long as they want. And if you think it's harder for them to live their life there, then too bad. You need to make peace with the fact that this is not about you. They have the right to live their life the way they want to." … And she was right.

It was one of those moments, and there have been many, when Tammy has confronted my way of thinking about something, my way of helping, my way of being, my way of doing what I believe is the "right" or "best"

thing for someone else. I learned Parallel Planning in what I believe is one of the worst moments of my marriage. And yet it contained, as bad times often do, a great gift and a great insight.

◇ PARALLEL PLANNING ◇

Again, *Parallel Planning* is making plans for our own lives while we walk alongside others who can't or won't make plans with us or as we wish them to. It's a way for us to ensure we can help those we love, if they want help, while simultaneously protecting ourselves. I've worked with many folks — both individuals and couples — on developing a Parallel Plan for a variety of potentially high-risk situations that would inevitably impact them in one way, shape, or form. These plans were made without the involvement of their loved one(s) simply because their loved ones weren't willing to acknowledge much less talk about the potential high-risk situation. Creating Parallel Plans allows you to be who you want to be in the lives of your Core Relationships with more autonomy and certainty in your own life.

I don't know about you but I like certainty, and life doesn't offer a whole lot of certainty. But when it comes to planning ahead for what we do on vacation, how we spend money and how we prioritize the material things and experiences our family wants, I like having some sense of control and ability to know what's next. Parallel Planning allows that. It definitely came as a gift to both me, and to Tammy and me as a couple.

We began to tell her parents what we could and could not do to support them while they lived in Texas and we lived in North Carolina. This invited them to participate in the conversation as they wanted, without the expectation that we needed them to do more than they wished or that we'd do more than we wished. As a result of our conversations, we were able to plan for the time and money to enjoy visits to Abilene that included us helping them in practical ways.

Lastly, Parallel Planning allows you to add people to your plans on your own terms. My plans were primarily made with my wife. It included my sons and others, but most of the planning was done by Tammy and me. By owning the process of Parallel Planning, you'll achieve your own clarity, which makes it a lot easier for others to enter the conversation when they're ready. To avoid making your Parallel Plans into demands, use the skills I've just introduced.

THE STAGES OF ESSENTIAL CONVERSATIONS
DISCOVER • DETERMINE • DEFINE • DELEGATE

Conversation by definition is an informal exchange of ideas via spoken word. Skillful conversation leads to enriched relationships, informed problem-solving, and shared decision-making. If you are really good at conversing — that is, if there is authenticity and transparency in a conversation — you can discover not only one another, but how to be in one another's lives. The Essential Conversations tool was designed to help guide your conversations and includes these four stages: *Discover, Determine, Define, and Delegate*. Remember, you're having these conversations with your Core Relationships. I encourage you to keep the list small as you begin. It may only be one, two or three people, and then let it grow from there.

DISCOVER

The first stage is *Discover*, and the goal is simple: to Discover one another within the Life Story and Life Compass frameworks. Sometimes, the people you're closest to are people you already know a lot about. But it's amazing what you'll learn when you sit and actually listen to someone *you think you know well*, saying in effect, "This is who I am, these are who my People are, this is the Place where I want to live my life, and as I look forward, here's where I see my life going."

The Discovery phase isn't something that happens all at once. It's a process that we repeat over and over with our Core Relationships. I know when I talk about this with my sons, I like discovering the people who are important to them. I like knowing who they process life with. I like knowing their Thought Partners. I like knowing the people that will be part of my life because they are part of their lives. Even though their friends may be much further from the center of my life in the concentric Circles of Connection, they are nonetheless there. Then, when we're together, I have a lot more capacity to be with their friends and deeply appreciate the gift they are to my sons. Learning about and sharing the significant people in each other's lives is such a gift! It's all right here in *discovery*.

I listen to discover where they are now and where they want to be in the future, and share where I am now and where I want to be in the future. As you go through this process, use your LERA skills and focus on "starting in the now." By discovering one another, you are learning what you need to know in order to be with each other, to come alongside one another, to give the gift of being in a relationship with one another, to mutuality, to interdependence. It all begins with being as authentic and transparent as you can be. This Discovery is the first step.

DETERMINE

The second stage we call *Determine*. This is when you Determine how you want to be in one another's lives.

In this stage, you will work to have a Shared Life Vision with the people you are with.

A Shared Life Vision is a way to describe the life you want to create together. This will enable you to choose how you want to be with people. As you continue your Essential Conversations, you can compose a description of your hopes for the ways you will support one another now and in the future. It will also inform how you want to include the others in your Core Relationships. Remember that each of the people you will share life with has a unique tribe in their Core Relationships. Sometimes you are making space for the same people. But this can be especially helpful when your work and relationships do not include the same people and need to have significant time and resources in order for you to flourish. You can imagine having a close friend who makes your life rich, yet they are not nearly as important to your life partner or Family of Choice. You can also imagine how important work relationships can be without those relationships being significant to the people in your Family of Choice.

For example: I worked with a couple seeking to set boundaries with their careers and the people in their Family of Choice. Their experience was one of letting the needs and requests of others invade their potential to love and support one another the way they wanted. I challenged them to form a clear Shared Life Vision, beginning with their commitment to each other as life partners, and let that guide how they make their time and resources available to the other commitments they have made. They came to see the value of having this clarity in each of their Circles of Connections. This process made sure the Outer Circles did not deplete what they believed was essential to keep their relationship rich and primary. This is not an exact science. It is not intended to restrict spontaneity or an openness to the shifting nature of work and relationships. They discovered that having this clarity allowed them to flow with the dynamic opportunities found at work and their other treasured relationships in harmony with the hopes that could only be realized in their relationship with each other. Once they had identified the characteristics and activities they wanted to protect in their life together, they were able to enter the adventures shared in those other places with other people while creating less resentment. It also gave them the experience of choosing a shared future that could include more of their unique Life Compasses.

Essential Conversations will involve the people needed to create a Shared Life Vision in each Circle of Connection. There will be times when those conversations are brief, especially as you work your way from inside out. There is more need for depth and clarity in our Core Relationships. Please do not make this into a laborious work that reduces the rich and adventurous elements of the relationships you enjoy. And do not neglect the Essential Conversations that will keep you from having what you want most with the people you love.

The couple I mentioned took their Shared Life Vision and used it to budget time and money. One of them liked a predictable routine with details, and the other wanted space to follow opportunities as they arrived without causing the other to feel neglected. They were able to work out some things that stayed in their budget and calendar while using a weekly check-in to adjust their plans and reconnect to their Shared Life Vision. It did not eliminate the need to work through "stuff," but it is continuing to help them return to the relationship they are choosing to have in their Shared Life Vision.

Here are two questions to ask in the *Determination* step:
- How do we want to relate, now and in the future?

- Do we envision ourselves channeling our energy, time, and/ or money to help one another as we move forward?

I think these are important questions to ask anytime you sense that you are not determined to be in someone's life in the same way they appear determined to be in your life. While we may want to have a relationship with someone, it's another thing to Discover what we each want and if we're both Determined enough to follow through.

DEFINE

In the first stage, we discovered one another. In the second stage, we determined how we want to relate to one another in life. In the third stage, we *Define* the roles we'll play now and in the future. In this stage, I like to say, "We're moving from ideal-life dreaming to real-life planning." This movement from ideal to real is one of the gifts of the Life Compass Plan.

Before we go any further, I want to pause and revisit the reality that the need to do this work is fairly new in the human experience. Since we've deconstructed our communities that held traditions for a shared life that included all ages, having these conversations about where we fit in each other's lives and defining our roles can be confusing and even scary. The thought of committing our energy, time, and money to someone through every Life Stage can be overwhelming, especially since we don't have a clear blueprint of how that works in today's world. I know as I tried to engage my people in defining roles, I discovered I had many fantasies, many ideas and many expectations in those relationships. And I realized that many were naive and uninformed.

The reality of supporting one another to the best of our ability — we're just doing it without a plan and we are not ready when a Life Quake happens. As we've already discussed, we're not at our best when a crisis hits and the anxiety is ramped up. We may have friends or a faith community that deliver meals when someone is sick or there's been a death in the family.

And I'm sure most of us have gone to visit someone in the hospital or walked the dog and fed the cat of a neighbor or friend when they've had to suddenly leave to go care for a family member. This is great. The problem is it isn't sustainable over the long run. People who weren't intending to provide meals or walk a dog or feed a cat can only do these practical things for a short time. Their lives are full. Think about the people in your life who have faced a Life Quake. You were shocked when you heard and wanted to help, but how long did your help continue? If you're like most, you probably returned to your daily routine within a couple of days or weeks or so, right? There's no judgment. It's the way our society works. You may have been the one who had the crisis and found that you were flooded with messages from people asking how they could help. It was great, and you felt tremendous love, but it was a bit overwhelming, right? And I'm sure, a few weeks past the crisis, you were sure wishing those people were still around. By that time, you felt weird asking for help. Why? Because those people have their own lives and you don't want to be a burden.

This is why identifying who our People are and having these conversations is so important. While the Discover and Determine stages help us to dream and mindfully think together about how we want to share life, the Define stage is when the rubber meets the road. This is where we move into the challenging process of real-life planning. Our Life Story and Life Compass now get translated into exactly who we are to the people in our life. In defining roles, I'd like to suggest six key factors to consider that I believe will help us share life.

SIX FACTORS IN SHARING LIFE

Below are what I believe to be six important factors that impact our ability to share life:

1. Proximity or Connectedness
2. Life Stage
3. Financial Ability

4. Emotional Capacities
5. Needs
6. Responsibilities

The first is Proximity. In order to be who you want to be to someone in your life, in order to have the relationship you want, how much does Proximity matter? I include in this what can be called Connectedness. There are elements of being together that require being in the same space and sharing human touch or providing practical support in person. My experience is that, with technology, much of what is needed can be had without being physically present in the same space. Tammy and I found that, once we embraced technology, we could eat breakfast with our grand-children in California regularly and still have the long talks we like with our son, their dad. I am not proposing that was equal to the intimacy we have when they live close to our home, but I do not want to keep us from using everything available to maximize how we can be together in light of all that determines our locations in life.

The second is Life Stage. Not only the stage of life you are in now, but where each person in your Core Relationships is along that human journey. We will unpack Life Stages in the next chapter on Place, but, for now, my suggestion is that, when you sit with your Core Relationships, as best you can, put a Life Compass Plan together for the stage of life you're each in, and the two stages that are ahead. As you do that, you'll be informed not only by the resources you have today, which we'll talk about in the Life Planning section of this book, but you'll also be able to anticipate what is normal in terms of the progression of life. This will enable you to prepare for those, so when crises come, you are better prepared, and the normal progressions are not experienced as Life Quakes.

One of the things I was surprised by was that, in the areas in which we did not have a plan, we had crises that in reality were just normal life. People get old, people get sick, a certain number of people have car accidents and a certain number of people have other challenges in life, but if we plan for the Life Stage we're in and the two stages ahead in our conversations, then we can actually reduce the impact crises have and be prepared for them.

The third factor is Financial Ability, not only for yourself but for those you're talking with. What are your financial resources now and what will they be in the future? If you take on a role in the life of another person, it is reasonable — and I would say only fair — that you know how your finances will be expected to contribute to maintaining that role and how their finances enable them to be who they desire to be for you. Real-life planning insists on this.

Do they have a financial plan and can they be trusted to keep the commitments they make financially? Are you able to keep the commitments you make financially? Do you even want to have financial commitments in the present or in the future? Before the Life Compass Plan, I did not think about the reality that, when there was a crisis in the people's lives I cared about, I was going to spend the money that was needed without consulting our budget, without consulting the long-term needs of ourselves and the others we were committed to, such as our sons. There were consequences we're still dealing with today. So, it's good to think about the Financial Ability you have in the present and in those two stages ahead to participate as you wish financially in each other's lives.

The fourth is Emotional Capacities. How can you participate in the process and how can someone else participate in the process? This has to do with Life Stage. When my sons were minors, they could participate in one way; now that they're adults, they can participate in another. But here, I want you to consider that people have limits emotionally, in terms of their own maturity, and even their educational and intellectual capacity to consider the factors that you might be considering as you have your Essential Conversations and work on a Life Compass Plan together.

It is important to respect one another's Emotional Capacities. Don't put expectations on someone that they're not able to meet financially or in their own personal life, emotional state, and the array of relationships and responsibilities they bring to the process. I call our attention back to the Trajectory of Readiness, as well.

So, there's Proximity, Life Stage, Financial Ability, and Emotional Capacities.

The next factor to consider is Needs. In light of the roles you consider taking in people's lives, take a realistic look at their Needs. Notice as you're having your Essential Conversations, who in your Core Relationships actually Needs emotional or practical support now. And what do you anticipate their Needs to be in the two stages ahead? Right now, Tammy and I have grandchildren, and our grandchildren need support. Our sons and their wives are parenting, and we want to support them in their parenting, and so we plan our lives around the way we want to support them. That is a joyful example. But there are also the hard realities that come as we age and Life Quakes happen.

You may have people who need support now and won't later, like the ways my sons needed support when they were minors, and don't need it now. But also think about how people will need support in the future. I have learned that some of what we were surprised by as our parents aged could have been predicted if we had spent the time having our Essential Conversations and making a Life Compass Plan.

The sixth factor to consider is the nature of the Responsibilities we each have in our work and the relationships with the others in our Core Relationships, or Family of Choice. Remember, this is true for each person and it expands out. So, in addition to how the person you're talking to fits into your life, you also need to consider how all those other people in your Core Relationships, your Family of Choice, fit into your life. We are not often responsible for other adults, but we would be served well by anticipating when that may occur and how we want to support them. Most of the work we do as we have our Essential Conversations and put together a Life Compass Plan is about choosing to be responsible *to* the people in our lives and providing some amount of emotional and practical support.

And then remember to pay attention to the people who are in the Core Relationships, or Family of Choice, of the people you support. Their people will be in your life, as well, to one degree or another.

I will share one illustration from our recent history. As my sons and their wives chose the couples that would raise their children if they were to die, sometimes called godparents, Tammy and I made the choice to know them better, because if what we hope will never happen actually happens, and either of my sons and their wives die, we want those people to know us well and be assured that they will have our support. When they took on the role of godparents in the lives of our grandchildren, they became the objects of our love and part of our Life Compass Plan. We now seek time to get to know people who live in New Jersey and Ohio because of a change in our sons' Core Relationships.

Those are Six Factors to remember as you have your Essential Conversations.

Another group to remember in our Essential Conversations is our Thought Partners. Thought Partners can actually be at different places in the Concentric Circles. In other words, someone in your family might also be your Thought Partner. It might be someone in your Joy Camp who is your Thought Partner. Have one or more people who are what we call a Thought Partner. Our Thought Partners help us discover what's true and good about our own lives, our own selves, and help us reflect on how we are in the world, how we live our lives, how we invest ourselves in other people. So, remember to keep Thought Partners as a defined role in your life.

Reflect on your Circles of Connection in every way in which you might want people to move in and move out, and recognize that movement as a natural, normal part of developing a Life Compass Plan. There's no need to judge yourself or others as you do that.

One more question to ask would be, "Do we want to stay in each other's lives for the long haul?" One of the greatest gifts we can have in life, as I mentioned earlier, is to have some relationships without exits. People who have decided to be with us for the long haul — to stay with us and to provide stability and security as we move through life. These people also help us have and maintain a perspective that includes all of life. And, if we're in it for the long haul, "How would we like to be together over the years that lie ahead?" I believe it takes planning in today's world to stay in someone's life.

Another consideration is how I will be to them and how they will be to me if there's a health crisis? When something happens, is this person among the people that will show up and help? How will they help? And, if they are, do they have everything they need to support you? Do you have everything you need to support them? In chapter five, on Protection, we'll talk specifically about how to make sure people have what is needed to be together and to help one another through a health crisis.

So once you have Discovered one another, once you have Determined how you want to be in each other's lives, and once you have Defined the roles that you want to have in one another's lives, the last step in Essential Conversations is to Delegate all that needs to be done in order to secure the ability to be what you have decided you want to be to one another. It is only as these are done that you can become confident that you can depend on one another and enjoy one another in the ways you want. A Life Compass Plan includes Essential Conversations as you begin and will continue with the people in your Core Relationships.

DELEGATE

Delegate is often the step where people want to start. As we talked about in the section on LERA, we often want to start with an Action before we Listen, Empathize and Reframe. It is tempting to start with our ideas about what we need to do. Instead, we're suggesting that these earlier steps of Discover, Determine and Define inform this step of Delegating. They also provide a way to reflect on the conversations we have so that when we need to Rediscover, Redetermine and Redefine, we notice it sooner rather than later. I have experienced and caused the anxiety that comes from unmet expectations, non-negotiated demands and unwelcomed help and advice. Now, I am better able to let go of the anxiety and return to the responsibility and gift of having my Essential Conversations, so everyone's Life Compass is honored and we help one another's Life Stories produce legacies of our own choosing.

Delegating can be assigning who will collect the information needed, provide care, arrange for the needed legal documents, or make the schedule of who will do what and when around a new baby or a dying parent. The examples are as practical and varied as all that is needed to fulfill the roles you wish to have in one another's lives.

WHEN TO USE MEDIATION

Now, not everyone is willing to be on board and ready to help in building a Life Compass Plan. Not everyone has the capacity to have the conversations that we may want to have or even believe they are needed. In these instances, you may need the support of a trained professional mediator. Formal mediation can be a great gift when we're dealing with urgency, complexity, anxiety, or conflict, and trying to make decisions about how to share life in those situations. This is especially true when it involves a person with a condition that includes a great deal of complexity and/or large expenses and you need help learning all that is medically, legally, and morally expected of you.

Mediators have the skill of noticing certain factors in relationships that will help you navigate with less conflict and fewer leftover resentments. When I took my training as a mediator, I had underestimated the potential and the need for guided negotiations to ensure the full participation of each person and the creation of mutually satisfactory outcomes. I watched as my mentor in mediation, Mike Haswell, worked with a couple trying to navigate their divorce and do what was best for their children. When they began, they were furious with each other. Mike helped them stay calm and access their best tools of communication and respect. As the sessions progressed, they came to a place where they asked kindly for what they wanted and compromised willingly as they were able, creating an elegant plan that honored their separate lives and made their co-parenting evidence of their mutual commitment to love their children well. It was one of the most amazing examples of how resistance can be recognized as passion and hard positions can be appreciated as the fear and anxiety that comes when boundaries are breached or threatened. Mike did not tap into anything that wasn't already there. He simply helped them discover the potential they had for negotiation when they were calm and mindful enough to access what was there. In the case of dealing with an older person in crisis, it's good to know that there are mediators who specialize in elder mediation.

PEOPLE SUMMARY

We've covered a lot of ground in this chapter, starting with our greatest challenge as a society — we need people to survive but we've deconstructed our tribes that were once a support system that kept us secure. Now we're facing a growing crisis in our relationships and our ability to manage the epidemic of health issues caused by lifestyle choices and aging.

We focused on the Circles of Connection concept as a framework to reconstruct our tribe. Using the Circles of Connection, we're able to identify our Core Relationships, the people who we depend on and who depend on us to provide the most emotional and practical support in our lives. They include our spouse or life partner, certain relatives and our closest friends (aka Family of Choice). We then have our Key Relationships, the people we depend on, but not as if they were family. They include our Joy Camp. Key Relationships are the people we deeply value but their presence is more fluid, meaning they move in and out of our lives more easily, depending on life circumstances, such as a job change or a move across town or to a new city. During times of crisis, our Joy Camp members often provide a great deal of support to us, emotionally and practically. We sometimes even decide to move them into our Family of Choice. Then there are the people on the Outer Circles, who are often in our lives for a short time but make a lasting impact. For example, a teacher, mentor, spiritual director, or nurse. Our Circles of Connection change as our lives change. That's why *you* are the center-most sphere and why it's critical that you understand who you are as a Person.

As we explored our Circles of Connection, we talked about the difference between:

- Being responsible *to* and responsible *for* someone,
- Emotional support and practical support, and
- Compassion and empathy.

We also touched on our ability to accept life on life's terms — something I call our Trajectory of Readiness — and the three words that I believe help us the most as we build our capacity to accept life: Facts, Power, and Ability.

Last but not least, we finished up with Essential Conversations, a communication tool developed with my friend and colleague,

Dr. Amy D'Aprix. We use the Essential Conversations process to guide our conversations with our Core Relationships. With it, we seek to *Discover* one another's Life Compass ("This is who I am, these are who my People are, this is the Place where I want to live my life and, as I look forward, here's where I see my life going"), *Determine* how we want to be in each other's lives, *Define* the roles we'll play, especially during times of transition, and *Delegate* who will do what and when to put our plans in place and as needs arise. When we boil it all down, our Essential Conversations are the glue that holds our Circles of Connection, our tribe, together.

In the next chapter, we introduce the third and final element of a Life Compass. As you turn the page, rest in a space where you trust that this messy and tenuous life will become less chaotic and more secure as you patiently discover the Person you are bringing to life and the People you want to share real life with. As we do that, I believe we can choose our Place in the world well and have the experience of being home, even as we embrace the moments we share and embark on the next adventure.

CHAPTER 4

Place

"I'm going home.
Back to the place where I belong. And where your
love has always been enough for me."
— *Ellis Paul, songwriter; Chris Daughtry, singer*

We all share a desire to live in a place that feels like "home." A place that our mind revisits the instant we hear the distant sound of neighborhood dogs barking or smell the aroma of a summer dinner being prepared on the grill. A place filled with rooms where we find refuge and share our laughter and tears with others. Let's look at how we can use our Essential Conversations and Life Planning tools to stay in a place we call "home" throughout every stage in our lifetime.

LIFE COMPASS LIVING AT HOME

When we entered this world, we landed in a place and depended on people we didn't choose, our family of origin. Many of us have fond memories of those childhood moments, whereas others of us long for a home we have never known but want to believe is possible. I have friends who were orphans and are reluctant to even use the word "family." Many of their stories are ones of sheer survival — some moving from one foster house to the next and witnessing, even experiencing, things none of us should ever have to witness, much less experience. These memories and the stories we tell ourselves about them shape our lives. I have become convinced by my investigation and my own experience that, when our story and our contributions are valued, supported, and expressed in the place we live, it feels like a home, a place we truly belong.

Regardless of our situation at the beginning of life, we have the power to build a "home" throughout our lifetime with our Family of Choice. A place where we pour the foundation with our stories and conversations, frame each room with our purpose and significance, and lay each shingle of the roof with our shared resources. This home we build together protects us from life's potentially devastating storms and ensures that each one of us arrives in a place at the end of our life that we've chosen — not one that's chosen for us. Best of all, this home is portable, we carry it with us. For, you see, homes are not the structures we dwell in but the relationships we live in.

Homes are not the structures we dwell in but the relationships we live in.

It's true that I can be a bit idealistic at times, but I want to reassure you that I don't believe our relationships are neat or within our full control. When I was young, I remember the years my dad was in Southeast Asia during the Vietnam War. He would reach out to us for short calls and say, "I shut my eyes here and I go back home. Hearing your voices reminds me of who I am." My dad's Life Story and contribution included the challenges we faced when he returned home and began the next part of his career and family life. There were power struggles between him and my mom and power struggles between the two of us. We didn't have the tools to work through them well. At times, his anger was explosive and his words were demeaning. I'm glad for the professionals who helped me take more responsibility for my life and emotions. They also taught me about the impact of war on those who return and do their best to reintegrate in their homes. As I learned from those experiences, I vowed that my life and future home would include the tools to work through anger without verbal or physical violence. As Tammy and I built our home, we had help from our faith communities and others in creating a place where we try to share mutual respect and value everyone's story and contribution. Tammy and I made the decision to build houses that included space for my parents. This was far from easy. By inviting them in, we were also inviting Dad's anger in, along with his way of expressing it. It took a lot of work to establish clearer boundaries for us all. I did my share of crossing boundaries and adding the toxic ways of my own struggles and stubborn hypocrisies. I share this story simply to reiterate that any "home" we choose to build within the context of our Life Compass Plan will be far from perfect. In fact, it will be riddled with all the messy and tenuous drama that comes with being human. What emerges, though, is the sacred ability to shape and savor our growth into personal responsibility and our legacy as a whole.

EMBRACING AGING/SENESCENCE

As we talk about our lives and building the place we call "home," it's important to talk about the process that happens between the moment we enter this world and the moment we leave it — aging. The scientific word for the process of getting older is *senescence*. Whether we like it or not (and most of us don't), aging is a fact of life. The good news is we get to decide *how* we do it.

Senescence involves a biological process that occurs at a cellular level that's initiated before we're even born. During this time and up until our mid-20s or so, our cells grow and expand like crazy. Then, the growth stops. At that point, we slowly begin to see and feel the impact this has on our body. We start to notice a few lines around our eyes, a gray hair here and there, and the sound of our knees crunching when we stretch. During our 30s, 40s, and 50s, we joke about "getting old." When we experience stiffness getting out of bed in the morning or pulling a muscle from merely picking something up off the floor, it's not that big of a deal. Then, in our 60s and beyond, it's not so funny anymore. We may still outwardly joke about it, but inwardly it starts to get scary. Things literally start breaking down, and we become acutely aware of all that we're losing. We will eventually lose our balance, our ability to see as clearly, to hear as acutely and to respond as quickly. Our hair thins, our nails become brittle, many of us gain weight, especially around our middle area, our skin thins, starts to sag, and bruises more easily, and we often lose our sex drive. We also start to realize that our kids — who used to call us all the time and ask for our input — don't seem as interested in our opinions. And employers who can hire younger, less-qualified candidates for less money stack our resumes in the "To Be Shredded" pile without a second glance. No wonder it's scary, right? The further we get away from our date of birth, the closer we get to the finale of our Life Story, where we face off with mortality. Some of us invest heavily in anti-aging creams, Botox and face lifts. Others buy sports cars, ditch their older friends for younger ones, and even have affairs. All in an effort to avoid the reality that time is passing and taking our youth with it. The reality is we can run as fast and as far as we want, but we'll never outrun this truth: Our life has a beginning and an end, and in between is aging — this thing called senescence. It's good to know that aging is a normal part of life. It's good to know that it's appropriate to learn to walk around age one. It's good to know that there's a time when you can begin to form sentences. An era when you can begin to create your own stories and be a Person in your own story. It's good to know that you have a season when you can become the best tennis player or the best baseball player or the best ballerina you can be. But there will come a time when you can't continue in certain endeavors, simply because of the normal process of aging.

Our Western culture's obsession with youth and disdain for growing old hasn't always been this way. We used to hold sacred reverence for our elders and deeply value their hard-earned insights. Unfortunately, with the dismantling of our tribes, we've lost our way. Now, as we grow older, some of us carry shame about our grey hair and wrinkles. We avoid talking about the aging and dying process like the plague. As we age, we feel less connected, less needed and less valued. And most of the kids in our world today only see Grandma and Grandpa once, maybe twice, a year. German-American developmental psychologist and psychoanalyst Erik Erikson believed that our fear of aging limits our ability to live a full life and, truthfully, I couldn't agree with him more. It's up to us to incite a paradigm shift in the way our children and their children view the process of being born, growing up, growing old, and dying, and that shift in perspective begins with us changing our view.

I want to suggest that aging is something we can help one another do; we can celebrate our children as we instruct them, enthusiastically welcome new people into adulthood as we equip them with the tools and the opportunities to access the shared dignity of our humanity as well as meaningful work, and then help those of us who continue as adults to become elders. I use the term "elder" to mean those people who hold the stories and places of honor in their communities and are seen as sources of wisdom. Humanity needs those who embrace the aging process rather than fight it. We benefit greatly from those who can teach us how to surf the tsunami of change without letting go of the essential lessons and virtues needed to live and love well. One of my childhood heroes was Bobby Allison, a legendary NASCAR driver. I got to meet him when I was 12 years old, and he was very kind to me as I told him why he lost his last race. I was sure it was NOT because the other driver was better. He was the best in my opinion. He just took the pit stop two laps early. He had a good chuckle as I shared my wisdom. There came a time when he retired, and he did not retire because he forgot how to drive a car. He retired because his response time — his ability to drive the car instinctively and respond quickly — was diminished. At that point, he entered into another role on his race team. It is normal to occupy a certain place in the first half of life. And there's also a very natural way in which we participate in the second half of life.

Getting old is part of staying alive, but every stage of life needs the wisdom that lets each of us do what is ours to do at that particular time in our lives. Elders may be older in years, but years are not the qualifier. I see young adults coming to wisdom much earlier than I did on my journey. When we see the human adventure from the center of our Circles of Connection and let the elders inform us, we turn aging into a collaborative process, from cradle to grave. Getting old is mechanical. Becoming an elder is a mindful process of maturity, compassion and service. The sooner in life we grasp the reality of senescence, the sooner we can make wise lifestyle choices.

As we explore the reality of aging, it's important to distinguish the difference between lifespan and life expectancy. **Life expectancy is what we can anticipate.** Each cohort, each group of people, each family, each culture, and each community can have different life expectancies. For example, my grandparents lived into their 80s; if I have a life plan that's any shorter than that, I'm not paying attention to my life expectancy. With the advancement of medical care, I really need to have a life plan that lasts through age 100!

Lifespan, on the other hand, is what's actually possible. It's possible to have a long life expectancy and make lifestyle choices that shorten your life. It's equally possible to have a shorter life expectancy and make lifestyle choices that extend your life.

When I speak to groups about this material, I often ask the question: "If you could take a pill every day that would reduce your chances of having dementia, reduce your chances of falling, reduce your chances of a heart attack, reduce your chances of disabilities, would you take that pill every day?" So far, in my seminars, it's been fairly unanimous. Everyone has said they'd take that pill every day. And even pay a fairly high price for it. Unfortunately, there's no magic pill. However, if we incorporate **the four elements** of human flourishing in our daily lives — practicing mindfulness, enjoying secure and mutually supportive interdependence in our Core Relationships, and maintaining physical and mental vitality — we're less likely to become debilitated and more likely to live long, die short, love well, and leave a beautiful legacy.

WE'RE ALL IN THIS TOGETHER

One of the cultural shifts that I'd like us to think about is a move from *aging in place* to *aging in community*. There have been many people who have wanted to stay in the same house, stay in the same town, stay in a specific geographical location. But what we're discovering is, often this fixation has an exacting price. It often doesn't get us what we *really* want or the support we need.

Humans actually seek to age in a community. When we define the community we want to inhabit at each stage of our lives, and the people that we wish to share our lives with, we can be more agile in our planning. When we're brittle and inflexible, insisting on yesterday's dreams of the "good life," we can inadvertently limit ourselves. One of my favorite quotes from Dr. Amy D'Aprix is this: "Your palace can turn into your prison if you don't do appropriate planning to make sure your home continues to match your needs and wants." Unfortunately, I've seen many people experience this. We lose our community and our ability to flourish when we age with rigidity.

I suggest we think about life and aging as an adventure. Adventures are exciting, remarkable, and often dangerous. The best ones are chosen, and those who share them bond deeply. Let's look at where we set up our base camp and become able to camp where we choose as long as we need to. As long as we can flourish there. As long as the people we want are there. As long as our story and our contribution are valued and find expression there. As long as we can serve others and play a part in a story bigger than ourselves there. In the midst of doing this, we experience the kind of living that keeps us positive and healthy, and not only shapes life, but actually empowers us to create and have the life we want and need.

You may be thinking, "Yeah, being on an 'aging adventure' sounds great, George, but where does money fit into this?" That's a great question. We all long for the dignity of work and a way to contribute. This is often connected to the income we need to support ourselves and our Family of Choice. It's true that our economy is changing, and many adults seeking a living wage are finding it harder. And there's a time when we may not have the physical health to work as we have in years past. Our responsibilities change as we go through life. Our abilities change. I'm suggesting that, through our Essential Conversations, we first establish who wants to share the adventure with us, then clarify our roles, and *then* creatively work to map out where we set up camp and how we pay for it. Some may decide to share a house, like we did with my parents. Others may decide their base camp won't actually be within the same structure but will be close enough that practical support is easy. My point is simply to introduce us to a useful way of thinking about aging — together.

LIFE STAGES

As we begin the adventure of growing old together, I'd like to give us some handles to hold onto as we blend our Life Stories and build our Life Compass Plan. These handles provide a way to better understand where we and the people we love are on the path of aging.

In the first half of life, there is important work to be done that can only be done during this period of time. I would argue that it's not a full life if you don't do the work of the first half of life, where our Life Compass is defined and implemented, and we reach the peak of productivity.

In the second half of life, we have a collection of insights from the first half of life. These insights come in very handy as we face the limitations and diminishing capacities that come with aging. The preparation we've done in our first half of life enables us to work smarter, not harder, and helps those in stages behind us gain wisdom that we've paid a huge price to collect. We can also access the relationships and resources we have enriched and accumulated in the first half of life.

I've given each of the stages a name but you don't have to be "married" to the name if you think of a better word. When you're talking to those in your inner Circle of Connection, by all means use whatever word resonates most with you. These were informed by some research but are not intended to do anything more than offer signposts for life's progression so we can look together at where we are and how we can help one another flourish all along the continuum. I'll dive into some of the motivations that energize each stage and then invite you to reflect on what it would mean to care for and support someone in that stage. Remember that the actual motivations and hopes of your People will be discovered in your Essential Conversations.

First Half of Life

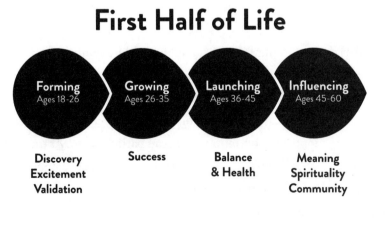

| Forming | Growing | Launching | Influencing |
| Ages 18-26 | Ages 26-35 | Ages 36-45 | Ages 45-60 |

Discovery
Excitement
Validation

Success

Balance
& Health

Meaning
Spirituality
Community

STAGES OF THE FIRST HALF OF LIFE

Drawing on the research of developmental psychologists, I've identified three stages in the first half of life — focusing solely on the stages of adults, starting at age 18, and/or those who are legally able to act as adults, acknowledging that this is something of a moving target. As we noted earlier, research indicates that active *adulting* is actually something that happens more often at age 24 or even later in our culture today.

Forming

Forming is the "adult horizon." In this stage, we find people between the ages of 18 and 24 who are motivated by discovery. Now that they've reached the threshold of adulthood, they're in "seriously seeking mode." For the most part, they have the capacity to make adult decisions; they get to discover who they actually want to be and how they actually want to live their lives. As we know, this stage in life involves a lot of training and a lot of trial and error.

People in this stage are also motivated by excitement. They're free in ways they've never been before and looking for something that's worth investing their life and time in. With that said, they're appropriately focused on experiences, so they can create meaning in a life that is theirs. Fortunately, and sometimes unfortunately, our expanding culture gives them more and more experiences to choose from. As they encounter these life experiences, they may or may not embrace the meaning given to them by their family of origin, culture and faith tradition — the matrix that brought them into this world and raised them to the point of turning 18 and beyond. Either way, they're also on the hunt for validation and a place to belong, a supportive community they can participate in. At times, their choice of community isn't necessarily healthy or wise. For example, it's not surprising that one of the things we're observing with the rise of cults and gangs is the search for *validation.*

The bottom line for this stage is that each Forming adult is going to choose a place where their story and their contributions are valued and expressed. In the absence of healthy authentic connection, they will chase excitement and validation in spaces that are not helping them flourish and/or empowering them as healthy members of the human family. When surrounded by a tribe that embraces them in this stage and applauds their efforts to discover and find the meaning life has in store for them, there's Magic! These young adults have such HUGE potential in themselves and the expanding capacities of technology, connection, and education. I am thrilled with much of what I hear them hoping for!

As this stage ends, we finish forming a workable adult version of ourselves, or at least approximating it. Our identity gets clearer and our values are formed and owned by us. These may be the values and community we've received from those who shaped us, but they become ours. And then we find a way to have significance. We find purpose and a place where our contribution is valued.

If you're in your second half of life, how can you support someone who's forming? I suggest you offer them encouragement to find their passions and discover the excitement in their lives. You'll also want to offer them validation that is healthy rather than toxic and helps them find who they really are, their true selves. For example, I was talking with a young adult who was asking me about a choice they were making. I said, "Well, why don't you talk to 10 people who made that choice in the past? Ask them how their lives are now and where their lives are going. Find out if that choice is one that you want to make." Later, we reconvened our conversation, and they began by saying, "OK, I've made my decision, and I'm not gonna do it. I took your suggestion. I asked some people how their lives were and where their lives were going. And I realized that choice won't take me where I want to go."

Remember, Forming adults won't communicate, connect, and work like past generations, so it's important to seek to understand how things are different for them and find common ground to meet them on. One book that gave me a view into the reality of the young adults I care about is *Connecting Generations: Bridging the boomer, GenX, and Millennial Divide* by Hayim Herring. We need to help one another flourish rather than demand conformity to anything that is past its time. Forming adults have much to offer folks in their second half of life, especially in being able to use the latest in technology and not miss the wave of progress. As we develop and invest in relationships with those in different Life Stages, we find that success is defined together and not in isolation.

As we expand in maturity, we move from Forming to **Growing.**

Growing

The second stage in the first half of adult life, **Growing**, occurs between age 24 and 40. In this stage, if you have indeed done the work of Forming, you're looking to succeed as the person you've chosen to be. You are striving to provide for yourself and those you love. And you define success as being able to find your way in life and provide for the life you want.

Obviously, we will continue to grow in many ways during this season. That's why Growing is an action word. Our identity will continue to grow and shift. And, if we're learning, there will not only be versions of ourselves that we hold onto and let go of, there will be people in our lives who enter and exit. There will be jobs that we do that become the jobs that we used to do. As our culture has become more transient and dependent on evolving technology, it's not uncommon for people to have multiple jobs and even careers as opposed to working for one company their whole life. People in the Growing stage are wanting to succeed in work, relationships, personal growth, and a host of hobbies and pet projects. One way to support a person who is Growing is to help them define success. Another is to help them succeed. When we don't do the work necessary to define success well, we can end up succeeding at something that fails to support all aspects of our Life Compass.

In our Essential Conversations we can explain to our Family of Choice how we plan to succeed and ask them to help us do so. As we explain and ask, we will refine our definition of success and help those we care about share in our plans. One of the biggest regrets people have at the end of life is, "I wish I'd had the courage to live a life true to myself, not the life others expected of me."[9] I'd like to suggest that many of the greatest regrets confessed by people late in life could be avoided if we helped one another, at this stage in life, to define success in ways that will motivate us for a lifetime and create a legacy we are proud to leave. It will help if these definitions are informed by elders we admire and want to emulate.

It is also good at times to refuse to help people succeed in ways that are toxic to themselves and others. Addiction is an obvious example. Active addicts often fixate on plans that are part of their slavery to the chemical, behavior, or relationships that are stealing their lives and could ultimately kill them. I am not inviting judgmentalism. That builds walls between us. I am encouraging us to talk about our lives and where they are going so we give compassionate consideration to how we support one another. We can slow down during our Essential Conversations and let wisdom and compassion guide us. There are times when we may want to let people we love learn from the pain that unfolds in their toxic plans. We can choose to use our resources in other beneficial ways or save resources to have them available for the healthier plans they make later. We will define and seek success in every stage of life, but in this stage, we are moving toward success in some of our most vital years.

Launching

The third stage in the first half of life is **Launching**. This typically happens somewhere in one's late 30s and early 40s. While it takes place in somewhat the same time frame, it comes after Growing. And it goes on until you've really reached the peak of your physical and professional life. In the midst of the Launching stage, people are looking for some sense of balance. They may battle with workaholism and spend a great deal of time and effort seeking a time management or productivity system. They're looking for a way to maintain or regain health while making the most of the years they have available. They want to maximize their capacity to work and support their Family of Choice through Life Transitions, like the kids going to college or the company downsizing. They're also beginning to get serious about what they want their life to look like when it's possible to slow down and reduce the load they are carrying. Oftentimes, if they're getting older and they have not moved beyond Growing, they will be chasing unrealistic ideas of success that are toxic to themselves and the lives they want. I have heard myself and others in this stage say some version of, "This pace is killing me, and I need to manage my money, time, and energy better."

One of the heroes in my journey is scholar, theologian, and social activist Thomas Merton. He has been quoted as saying, "People may spend their whole lives climbing the ladder of success only to find once they reach the top that the ladder is leaning against the wrong wall." Living in alignment with our Life Compass helps us know when our ladder is on the wrong wall and can guide us using our "true north." This is even more reason for us to be passionate about each person intentionally crafting their own Life Compass as early as possible. Knowing who we are as a Person, who our People are, and the Place we'll set up our base camp throughout our Life Stages is a way for us to transform the common experience of a midlife crisis into a shared midlife adventure. Shared adventures often change direction but they don't have to include losing ourselves or the people we love along the way. The more we invest in the place we share with each other — our local communities and our homes — the more we'll realize the potential that is held in both halves of life. We won't end up living our lives in a way that ends with a song of lament. The lament is not just for those of us who are older. I've met young adults who are lamenting their lives. Young people seek self-definition, secure relationships, and a place of significance. And yet, they're finding it frustrating. They have many social connections, but it is hard to find the kind of connections that actually encourage humans to live into the best versions of themselves and help one another do the same.

There's a lot that goes on in the first half of life, Forming and Growing and Launching. And as we move into the second half of life, we'll carry all that inspired us in the first half. We will continue to discover and be motivated by curiosity and ingenuity. We will continue to seek excitement and live in harmony with our passions. If we are going to flourish, this must be true. We'll always need validation on some level. But, as we get older, we don't live just for the validation of others, nor do we live just to make money. We find deep satisfaction as we give our lives for the sake of something bigger and clearer that will include the generations behind us. We want to succeed, but we redefine success in light of what we've been learning — not only in our own lives, but in the history of humankind on the Earth.

The reality is that we seek health, and we're seeking it in new ways. I remember back in the 1980s, when people were recovering from hip surgery and they were given days to lay still and recuperate before they started moving. Now, people have hip surgery and are home in a day or two — and this actually turns out better. They heal more completely. So we're learning about how to be healthy. We're learning about how to spend our time on what helps us flourish. We do best if we live intentionally and vitally in the first half of life while we anticipate and prepare for the second half of life while learning from the people who are already there.

STAGES OF THE SECOND HALF OF LIFE

The focus of the first half of life is appropriately on Forming ourselves, Growing and running experiments in how to succeed. Next comes the hard work of using the health we are able to maintain as we chase the potential of the work and relationships we choose. Our people actually need us to do this work. As we enter the second half of life, an interesting shift begins to happen. I liken it to the shift that occurs in a long-term relationship — when we begin to feel more settled, more comfortable. Part of this shift occurs because our motivations are changing. We've walked through many life experiences and transitions that have impacted us in profound ways. By this season in life, many of us have witnessed the birth of our children and the death of our parents. We've had friends die young of cancer and car accidents and even suicide. And some of us have struggled with our own health issues. We've climbed the hill that sometimes felt like a mountain, and we want to plant our flag to memorialize that we made it. This flag symbolizes that our life has meaning. Here, we decide how to write the rest of our Life Story and how we wish to shape the legacy we will leave. We are learning to live mindfully as we settle into a deeper, larger, higher plot line that guides the time we have left in our Life Story.

Second Half of Life (Eldering)

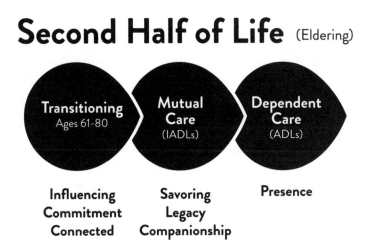

Transitioning
Ages 61-80

Mutual
Care
(IADLs)

Dependent
Care
(ADLs)

Influencing
Commitment
Connected

Savoring
Legacy
Companionship

Presence

Influencing

The initial stage in the second half of life is one I call **Influencing**. It unfolds, on average, between ages 45 and 62. In this stage of influencing, you're motivated by *meaning*. In other words, being able to tell the story of why you live your life. It's less about what you do and more about why you do it. It's less about doing it for yourself and more about doing it for others and for something bigger than yourself. As such, we enter into different conversations at dinner parties — talking politics, current events, and swapping concerns about our kids entering high school or leaving for college, and our parents needing more and more assistance. Sometimes we're going through a divorce, entering widowhood, going through the stressful adjustment of an empty nest, or facing a shift in our professional lives for various reasons, some that may not have been our choice. It's during this stage that we begin to frame our lives inside of a community larger than our Family of Choice. It might be a religious community, a retirement community, a neighborhood community, and/or a book or gardening club. The point is, we're now shifting from the demands of our younger selves into really understanding and valuing on a much deeper level our lives and our relationships. We're sandwiched between our kids and parents, and can clearly see the influence our lives have on both those younger and those older than us and our world at large.

Another motivator is *spirituality*. I'm not talking about the particular religion within which your spirituality takes shape. I'm not talking about whether you have a particular vision of a deity, or lack thereof. In spirituality, I'm naming the capacity to discover and live into a truer version of ourselves, living vitally in the world as it actually is. People who are spiritual, in the way I am using the word, are not avoiding reality. They are coming alive inside of reality. They are not asking to have a life, they are finding out how to live the life they have.

This is also the stage when we begin buying over-the-counter reading glasses for every table and drawer in our home, and get to experience the "joy" of preventive mammograms and colonoscopies. We don't experience the Fear of Missing Out (FOMO) like we once did, and most of us like to hunker down earlier in the evening. You won't find us ALL eating dinner before 5 p.m., but we definitely like to go to bed earlier on Friday and Saturday nights than we used to. It's not that we won't go out to listen to live music that starts at 10 p.m., it's just not as often nor as appealing. Inside, we may still feel like we're 20, but our joints and muscles are becoming acutely aware that they're nowhere near 20. I remember the realization that it would be best for me to stop playing softball with the young people. I was still holding my own, but my body and the desires of my soul were telling me there were ways to stay vital and build relationships that did not involve as much Advil and time away from my porch.

To support someone in the Influencer stage, first and foremost, share some conversations. Most people in this stage are carrying a heavy heart load and need more than anything to talk with those they share life with. They're also most likely carrying a heavy task load. Like I said, they're often balancing launching kids and caring for aging parents, which is one of the most challenging jobs out there. Validate their experience and offer practical help, like a dinner, a few hours of caregiving respite, or a massage gift certificate.

Transitioning

Transitioning, the next stage in the second half of life, starts around age 60 and lasts as long as our health and the vulnerabilities of mortality allow. It's one that unfolds in whatever way it unfolds. You begin to reflect not only on the influence you've had, but on the influence that's possible between this moment and the end of your life. You make peace with the Life Story you have lived (backstory), and come to see the past and the days left as precious gifts to be savored and shared. These years will include the work of applying wisdom to each day, as well as restoring and enriching our Core Relationships, This is often when we get serious about a "bucket list."

In this stage, we focus more on the motivator of *contentment*. As I've been entering this stage in my own life, I find great value in the time I spend on my porch. There are actually three porches on my house. When I was younger, I didn't see a need for a porch. But now, I believe the porch is the best space my house has. It's a place where I sit and I breathe deep. I think about the past and the present, and look into the future. It's where I have the joy of reflecting on the life I have shared with the people I've loved and reflecting on life with those I love now. I am rediscovering the joy of finding forgiveness for the ways I have not loved well. It's forgiveness that comes from others and something I offer myself. I seek contentment and, in transitioning, contentment is a motivator. Contentment is also sought along the way. I see hope that our current culture is focusing on the value of mindfulness and that it will not have to remain something found only late in life. In this stage, we're learning to ask: "How can I let go of what has been and own what is?" "How can I find peace in the midst of the real life I'm in and not demand a life that doesn't exist?" Contentment is worth the time it takes to be desired and found. At this point, we're more likely to make the time to find contentment and do the work on ourselves to listen deeply with a peaceful open mind to all the wisdom we can find.

Another motivator in transitioning is *connectedness*, or relatedness. We actually want to find contentment as we access, accept, and choose our place in the lives of others and the plot line that guides us. We share life with others with a keen awareness of how we support one another. We also seek a plan that enables us to navigate how all the forms of support we share in our Circles of Connection will be directed as we live the years we have left before aging starts to significantly change the way we can participate. We can embrace this stage and flourish as we continue to have our Essential Conversations and create a Life Compass Plan.

One of the things I have in my life is called Porch Time. I have some family and friends, young and not so young, who gather on the porch to talk. There's no formal agenda other than the invitation to ruminate, think, and talk about what we're finding in life while we remember and experience that we're in this together. These Thought Partners are important. Connectedness is not unique to this stage but it is more fully developed and a motivator that eclipses most of the others. It often means we choose fewer activities and relationships in order to know and share life in ways that can only be discovered with more time, trust, authenticity, and grace.

If you are wanting to support a person in this stage, let them know who they are to you. You may also be able to contribute to the work they are doing on themselves by sharing your own experience as part of their Life Story. It is a huge gift to have young people help them reflect on and shape the ways they are navigating the challenges of transitioning.

Recently my nephew called to request some porch time. When we got together, I took more of the time than usual. I shared my struggles and hopes. He honored me with his insights and some pushback on things that seemed to him to be out of touch with how our world is actually unfolding. The gift of himself and the honor of treating me like I can handle reality helped me find contentment. I am learning that I need not insist on the futile hope of real life going the way I want. This is one example of sharing life with a person who is committed to me and knows I am committed to him. We sat on the porch together, navigating through our messy, tenuous lives trying to maintain our authenticity, integrity, and mutual respect. He is who he is, I am as I am, and we are as we are. At this point, I want to spend as little time as possible on the things that hinder sharing life well.

MUTUAL CARE AND DEPENDENT CARE

After influencing and transitioning, the second half of life moves into the last two stages. I call them **Mutual Care** and **Dependent Care**. It is the time when our mortality is right in our face. It's the time when we realize we can no longer live the way we have with our full health and all our capacities. Some of us experience these as invaders we did not see coming, Life Quakes. Our hope in the Life Compass Living Community is to help one another experience them as transitions common to us all. We can navigate the new realities with elegance and even flourish in ways that are missed by those who do not embrace them and plan accordingly. We will still find life messy and tenuous, but we will reduce some of the vulnerabilities.

Some people live a long time in what I call Mutual Care, like people who have lifelong disabilities. They need some degree of practical support even as they make heroic efforts at doing all they can. They show us the beauty of doing and giving as they are able, while allowing others do the same.

Mutual Care

Mutual Care is not a stage to be avoided. It is a stage to be embraced. It's not something you desire, at least at the outset; you simply embrace it. And the difference is huge. No one likes being dependent on others and going through the progression that leads us to the end of our lives, but we can prepare ourselves to receive it. And we can understand that, inside of our community and Core Relationships, just as people need help as they are being born and are celebrated, we can be helped and celebrated as adults. And so we move to Mutual Care.

From my perspective, Mutual Care has two phases. The first I call **Companionship**. This phase is when you and those around you realize that you need to be checked in on, on a regular basis. It might be that you need to be called each day. You may not need help getting the trash cans to the curb each week or changing a light bulb that requires getting up on a ladder, but someone needs to notice if they don't get done. It might be that the person you're concerned about in this stage has had a little episode of confusion, has begun to isolate socially, or has begun to neglect personal hygiene. It's time to start paying attention to how they are doing and to reinforce their social support. The people in their Core Relationships can stay in touch, notice how they are doing and encourage them to flourish in the ways we have described.

There's great magic in this stage when the person in the companionship phase finds people coming around them. It is sometimes the case that a group of friends are in this stage together and become close by asking about each other, going together to activities and on outings. It is good to share stories of what's been happening recently and what the future holds. It's a good way to inhabit one another's lives. My dad and his Joy Camp checked in on one another. They'd let me know if they had concerns about Dad. It went the other way, as well. My dad expressed concern for friends, and we were able to experience the joy of helping them. This phase lasted for several years after Dad had a few health issues. He was still able to do all that was needed but he was slipping. I am forever grateful for those who loved my dad all that time.

When I was growing up, my family lived away from my dad's hometown of Donaldson, Arkansas. When we'd visit my grandmother, I can remember watching people come by to visit her in the house where she lived. Many of them were relatives who still lived in Donaldson. Others were simply neighbors. It was a constant check-in. I can imagine that, as my grandmother was going through what I call Companionship, no one really noticed anything extra being done because that community simply checked in on one another. It was just part of the routine to see how Ruby was doing on their way to the store. And some of her own children lived behind her and would walk by regularly. They shared many more meals than we typically do now. They shared more daily routines. There was no need to decide she had entered a new stage of life and no need to start doing anything different. It was good to know Grandma had support. Later, she had to move closer to some of her children who could care for her and, eventually, to a skilled nursing facility before she died.

By establishing and living in alignment with a Life Compass, I believe wholeheartedly that it's possible to build a life where checking in and being together is maintained in the natural flow of our days. It takes some effort up front to pay attention and plan all we need to plan, but the emotional, physical, spiritual, and financial return on our planning investment is priceless. For a variety of reasons, many of us isolate socially as we age. By this stage, we've become less mobile, and the people our age have become less mobile or perhaps have even died, which makes the number of people we're engaged with smaller. It's also true that we isolate socially because we don't have the attention, energy, and drive to be engaged as much as we used to. When this happens, our world literally becomes smaller. The younger people in our lives are busy and often spread out, and can easily forget to include us in their days. We often translate this to mean we're no longer valuable to them and they don't care about us anymore. It's been my experience that this is not necessarily true. Chances are high that there are people who absolutely do value you even though you feel socially isolated. Oftentimes, if they haven't heard from you, they make an assumption that you're as busy living your life as they are living theirs. By having a clearer understanding of the Companionship phase (and all Life Stages, for that matter), I'm hopeful that we'll pay better attention to the specific needs in this phase so we will show up for one another.

The second phase within the Mutual Care stage is known by needing help with **Instrumental Activities of Daily Living (IADLs)**. This acronym (IADL) is a clinical term used in the helping professions. It's a specific list of activities many begin to need help with.

Instrumental Activities of Daily Living include:
- Shopping
- Cooking
- Managing medications
- Communication (phone, email)
- House cleaning
- Doing laundry
- Transportation
- Managing finances

What will be done and who will get them done when you, or someone you support, needs help with these things?

When my father entered this stage, it was the first time that I actually became aware of his growing limitations. The Companionship stage was not as much something we needed to plan, because he lived with us. But he was able to hide, for a surprisingly long period of time, the fact that he was not managing his finances well anymore. And, while we used to check in once a month on how he was doing, he let it pass a few months, and I didn't think anything about it. When we finally sat down to become current, I realized he had made the choice to no longer balance his checkbook, which was a pretty big deal since he had taken such pride in doing it without fail. I realized that day that he had expenses in his checking account and on a credit card that he could not recall committing to.

We made the decision that I would do bookkeeping on his checkbook and his credit card, and we talked each week about what was showing up in those accounts and the choices he had made. This worked for a couple of years. In addition, he no longer wanted to do his laundry. My mother had passed away, and that had been her responsibility in their division of labor. For a while, he did his own laundry, then he started taking his laundry to a laundromat, where a person would do it for him. In this process, he made some friends at the laundromat. Not only that, but he also hired someone to come in once a week and clean his part of the house. You can see the progression that's happening. It was at this time I realized that I had to start paying attention to what my dad was able to do. We started talking more about his limitations, his mortality and how he would live into this progression that was ahead of us. These were Essential Conversations that informed some planning and helped my dad and me share this normal process of aging in ways I will always treasure.

When you're in the midst of Mutual Care and you go through the phase of Companionship, I suggest that you think ahead into the phase of IADLs, of needing some help but still remaining mostly independent. My dad's progression in this IADL phase of the Mutual Care stage lasted a few years, and he ended up needing help with everything on the list.

Mutual Care has motivations, tasks, and even gifts within it. Mutual Care can make space to savor life and reflect on your legacy. This is often when we finish work on the bucket list and discover it needs some significant edits. We also see the value of making amends, spending time with people and activities we value, and any number of things we desire as we're slowing down and facing mortality. It was indeed in those times with my dad, as well as in my years as a minister to people in this stage, that time was spent telling stories of the past. We would reflect on the people, experiences, joys, and regrets in their lives. They would also talk about what they would like to include in their lives as they moved forward. Some of them would also talk about how they were seeing their legacy, nourishing their innate desire to be part of something bigger than themselves.

In Mutual Care, it's a good time to collect and share the stories that brought us to this stage. There are many people leveraging today's new technology to discover their family history and even communicate with those they discover in their search. I celebrate every way we learn our stories and how our stories are connected. Please prioritize getting to know the lives and history of the people in your Core Relationships. Security and familiarity at the center of our Circles of Connection will increase our capacity to do Mutual Care. My dad was still helping me and others during those days. He just had to admit some limitations that gave us the joy of doing things for him.

I used a pack of cards called Caring Cards with my dad. These cards provide prompts for storytelling and proved to be very valuable. I would leave the cards with him, and he would work with them on his own, too. When people would come in to help, and they were wondering how to have a conversation, I would tell them to just pick up those cards and read one. They'd let him talk and then share their own stories the cards encouraged. One of the cards says, "What are some of the things you're most grateful for?" Another reads, "What volunteer work have you done?" Another asks, "Where did you live when you were a child? And how did your family come to live there?" So many of these prompted my dad to tell stories that

I never knew, and I regret now that I didn't record more of his answers. I now suggest that those working with the Caring Cards at any stage use the voice memo function on your phone or other recording device to collect responses to these questions as they're given. You can then curate these digital files and give them as a treasured gift to family and friends. They can also be a great introduction of your loved one to someone new in their lives.

When we enter Mutual Care, we're also being given the gift of our mortality. Mortality is often seen as the grim reaper, a dark, haunting figure that's come to steal you or someone you love. I've come to learn that death is not just the end but a beginning to the next journey of life. It calls us, no matter our age, to savor, to collect, and to reflect on what our life has meant to us and the people we love. As I began to have to take care of more of the things that my dad needed, I was drawn into the kind of relationship with him I longed for all of my life. Don't get me wrong. There were also many struggles and pains related to his diminished capacities. It was exhausting and incredibly stressful at times. I wish we had involved more people in his care team. I wish we had planned ahead better. That's part of why I'm writing this book. But do not miss the gift of each of these stages, particularly the last two.

Dependent Care

After Mutual Care comes **Dependent Care**. Dependent Care is the stage that takes us from this life to the next. The first and typically the longest phase of Dependent Care is **ADL, Activities of Daily Living**, where we need help with most aspects of our life. The average person spends two and a half years needing this level of support. It is the way we pass on our lives in the final coda we are living. The medical and aging community professions use the letters ADL.

Activities of Daily Living include:

- Bathing
- Dressing ourselves
- Grooming
- Oral hygiene — brushing our teeth
- Toileting
- Transferring ourselves from a bed to a chair, or into a car
- The ability to walk
- The ability to climb stairs
- The ability to feed ourselves

When we begin to need help with one or more of the ADLs, we are entering the stage of Dependent Care. This is the time when we cannot live a day without others being present and assisting us with what has to be done. When you need help with more than one ADL over an extended period of time, you are entering what is called long-term care. You will need to know how long-term care is different than the times we need help that are covered by medical insurance. At this point, it's important to recognize that when we're thinking of our Place, when we're on the adventure and planning the movement of our lives from one place of making ourselves at home to another, one of the things to think about is the reality of this stage of life I call Dependent Care.

The second phase of Dependent Care is **Hospice**. People enter hospice care when a physician formally pronounces that your prognosis is that you will die within the next six months. (Please confirm this definition in your location, since the specifics can vary.) Hospice is an amazing gift to many people and their families. They understand the end-of-life process and provide incredible support across the board — physically, spiritually, emotionally, and practically. I encourage you and anyone you may know who's in the stage of Dependent Care to consider the support found in a hospice designation.

There are at least two main reasons I suggest this. One is that having the wraparound support of a good hospice in your community will be very helpful, no matter how accurate your physician's timeline is. Almost everyone I've observed improves. The stress level of the caregivers goes down dramatically. And more people become involved and come around the person once the hospice designation has been given and hospice is involved.

The second reason is the experience of the one facing this transition. Many will want the support of palliative care. This is when medical support is focused on relief from the symptoms and stress of a serious illness. The goal is to improve quality of life for both the patient and the family without taking drastic measures to prolong life. Palliative care can be given in other contexts than hospice and for the treatment of conditions that do not qualify for hospice. I encourage us all to be aware of all the programs, products, and services available and use that support to have a role in our own living, loving, and dying.

Please do not spend any more time than is absolutely necessary in denial when it is time for you or someone you love to receive the kind of help that hospice offers. You may or may not want all the support that's available through hospice. It's completely up to you and your family, and you can direct the process so that you can have the experience you desire. The social worker, the chaplain, the nurse, the doctor, and the ready availability of all the supportive medications for pain relief — the entire, whole-person package — has been designed to ensure we have the support we need when we face the end of life. It's worth working through our insecurities and denial of our mortality to embrace this universal human transition.

If you're in the United States and enrolled in Medicare, your medical co-pays and deductibles are paid when you enter hospice. This can save a significant amount of money for many people. I encourage people to see hospice as a gift when it is time.

The motivator in this stage can be summed up in the word *Presence*. When we arrive at the end of our journey in this world, we want to be able to be present to ourselves and *for* ourselves so that we can consciously participate and be in charge as best we can. We want to know others are present, too. There is often a necessary difficulty found in managing what is done for comfort and the level of consciousness possible. It is very important, as we will talk about in the chapter on Protection, that people have their legal documents in place, as well as the designated people who will speak on their behalf in the event they can't do so themselves.

For now, let's remember that this last stage of the human journey can be very difficult. However, it can also be a huge gift to the person going through this final transition, as well as the people who come around them. When a baby is born, we celebrate the miracle of their birth and the beginning of a new life. At the time a person transitions "home," we celebrate the entirety of that person's life. We share stories about that person, recall with gratitude the contributions they've made to our lives, and, in some instances, offer grace and forgiveness.

Grace and forgiveness are shared offerings we must include if we are to be secure with each other as humans. We all do things that are indeed harmful and toxic. Ideally, we will find the capacity within us — in Dependent Care, and at every stage — to be present with one another and share what I believe to be the highest and most sacred gift of human existence: moments of complete vulnerability and authenticity, the moments when we are fully present with one another without the need to hide who we are or deny even the not-so-pretty facts of our lives. This has certainly been the case with my dad and others that I have companioned through the end of life. Once Dad's Alzheimer's diagnosis was joined by a Stage 4 lung cancer diagnosis, we recognized that we needed to be ready for him to die. I could tell many stories of the traumatic moments when he was filled with fear; we talked and cried together. I can say they were awful, and yet I am glad we were able to share those times. I hate thinking of what it would have been like for him to be in such terror alone. At one point, I laid down in the bed with him so we could share a hug. My mind went back to an evening when I was 8 years old and I fell asleep next to him after he returned from the Vietnam War. I was overflowing with emotion and my mind played scenes like a movie from the story of our lives. He was my dad, and I was his son. It was one of the most intense moments of gratitude this boy has known.

The intensity of those days led to one of the most precious moments of my life. Dad could not be kept comfortable, so we were about to move him to the hospice unit so he could have full medical support. He didn't have much energy left. He didn't spend a lot of time consciously interacting with the room around him. But he looked at me, and I looked at him. I said, "I love you." He said, "You're a good son." And so our communication ended, and my heart was flooded with a confusing crescendo of joy and grief worthy of our life together.

We moved him to the hospice unit, and he died 14 hours later. My brother-in-law, Robert, made his way to the hospice unit. He insisted on staying with me, and I was glad. Robert and I were there when my dad breathed his last. I will forever be bonded with my brother-in-law because of that moment. Presence is a huge gift at any stage in life. But in this last stage, it is what we hold onto. And if we would listen to the wisdom of the teachers throughout human history, we would recognize that — whether we're forming ourselves at age 18 or transitioning beyond this life at the end — the biggest gift we can bring and the greatest thing we can receive is someone's full

Love is an idea awaiting full expression until we are together, fully exposed, unashamed and eyes wide open to a shared horizon.

presence. Love is an idea awaiting full expression until we are together, fully exposed, unashamed and eyes wide open to a shared horizon.

PLACE — AT HOME TOGETHER

The ability to be with one another and respond according to what is needed in each moment and stage of life is the key to living out our Life Compasses. We can help one another discover and live into the best version of ourselves in each stage of life. We can know who our people are, our Core Relationships, in order to enrich those relationships now and look forward together at the vast landscape of this great adventure. With a Life Compass Plan, we'll be better equipped to let relationships transition in and out of our Circles of Connection with our eyes wide open. And we'll treasure the gift we are to one another. As we consider our Place in our Life Compass, we seek to live at home. And yet we must hold things lightly enough so that, when it's time to move along, we can go with all the furnishings needed to have some sense of home in the next place. Living at home in each stage of life is different. I hope that, in your Essential Conversations, one element you discuss is how collectively you can help one another to have the experience of *being home,* the experience of *belonging.* When I look around the office in which I'm writing this book, I know I belong here. The things on the walls and on the shelves are about my life. Pictures of people who are at the center of my Circles of Connection. In addition to where you live and what is inside that apartment or house or condo, there are the people that are with you. Often the biggest part of what makes a place feel like home is the people who can show up when you want them to, and when they're needed. The people you can show up for when you're needed. The people you can be with in a way that fits into your routine and the richness of your lived life. I can't tell you how grateful I am for the gift of technology that enabled us to eat breakfast on a regular basis with our grandchildren who were a couple thousand miles away. I'm even more grateful for the times when we're in close proximity. Remember, home will always include the ability to be with the people we want to be with, do the work we want to do, whether paid or volunteer, and know deep inside that we matter in this life.

PLACE SUMMARY

We've unpacked a lot of material in this chapter. First and foremost, we touched on the idea that our Place is not the actual physical structures we dwell in but our relationships we live in. We then moved into gaining a better understanding of the aging process, called senescence along with the physical, spiritual, and emotional challenges we face as we age in a society that doesn't value elders.

We then focused on the idea of growing old together as an adventure and using our Essential Conversations to engage our Core Relationships to join us. To do this, we need to understand stages we move through in both the first and second halves of life. The stages in the first half of life include Forming, Growing, and Launching. In the second half of life, there's Influencing, Transitioning, Mutual Care, and Dependent Care. If we look at life from a 30,000-foot view, we can see that the first half of life is about building the storyline of our Life Story, and the second half of life is about building how that story produces our legacy. Our legacy isn't just about the money and "things" we leave after we die. It's also about finishing the items on our "bucket list" and spending time with those we love.

In the remaining chapters, we'll talk about the Process of creating our Plan that will protect and provide for our Person, People, and Place.

Carl Jung said, "One cannot live the afternoon of life according to the program of one's morning. For what was great in the morning will be of little importance in the evening. And what in the morning was true will in evening have become a lie."

I hope that as we journey into the next section of the book, you will give whatever time is necessary to be clearer on who you are as a Person, seek clarity within, and have your Essential Conversations with the People you want in your life, especially in your Core Relationships. Then you will be better able to help one another have what you need to be at home together in your Place … and so much more!

CHAPTER 5

Planning

"Suffice it to say that something automatic and extraordinary happens in your mind when you create and focus on a clear picture of what you want." — David Allen

We've now arrived at the section of the book where we talk about how to have Essential Conversations and build a Life Compass Plan. We all want to live our lives to the fullest and be secure now and in the future with the people we love, but real life leaves us with vulnerabilities we can't ignore. Some are external vulnerabilities we have no control over, like a corporate layoff, a global pandemic, or an unexpected illness. And some are internal vulnerabilities, like the fears and anxieties that often develop early on in our lives. As I previously mentioned, these vulnerabilities can keep us from getting clear about who we are and what we want in life. Some of us may have an idea of who we are and what we want. Yet, for any number of reasons, we lack the ability or motivation to dedicate the time needed to work on ourselves and have our Essential Conversations; the conversations that will fuel the unfolding of our life vision in alignment with our Life

Compass. Regardless of the vulnerabilities or struggles you've faced to this point, the great news is you can start today. Remember, we're moving toward more security, more love, and more resources. And even the smallest step forward is a step forward.

> Remember, we're moving toward more security, more love, and more resources. And even the smallest step forward is a step forward.

Speaking of steps, every step you take toward having your Essential Conversations and creating your Life Compass Plan will have three big payoffs. The first is that you will become more secure. Each time you identify and meet a need, whether it's a current or future need, you will reduce the vulnerabilities that come with the tenuousness and the messiness of real life. For example, a friend called me the other day about her dad, who's in his 90s. She said, "George, what was the name of that form that I need to make sure my dad signs?" To which I replied, "Well, there are a couple of critical ones you need to get in place as soon as possible." When we hung up, I was proud of her for taking the step to call and ask. She's moving toward helping both her dad and herself gain more security as he moves closer to the end of his life.

Taking the steps necessary to ensure you have all of the paperwork in one place to protect yourself and those you love is an incredible relief. It also leaves you feeling greatly empowered and more secure. Note: as I've said before, this isn't just for people living in their last chapter of life. We need to have our affairs in order as early as 18 years old. To help folks with this, I've created what I call the First Folder Checklist. I've named it this because it's the first folder you'll grab in the event of a health crisis or death. I'll guide you through the First Folder Checklist in the next chapter.

The second big payoff is that your relationships are going to be more intentional and secure. In other words, you're going to know more about where you fit into the lives of people who are important to you and where they fit into yours. You'll look at and relate to one another on a deeper level. For instance, I remember a friend telling me that she couldn't imagine feeling closer to her best buddy from childhood. That is, until she asked her buddy to be her Health Care Power of Attorney. "It was like we had stepped into an even deeper part of a pool together," she said. "Now, I literally trust her with my life." That kind of trust is something money can't buy. Remember, we're moving away from a single focus on financial investments as a means of security throughout our lifetime. We're also choosing to include deep investments in our relationships.

The third big payoff is the progress you'll make on the Trajectory of Readiness (discussed in Chapter 3). Remember, the Trajectory of Readiness is all about building our capacity to accept life and be present and participate in it as it is — not how we want it to be or hoped it would be, but as it is. As you take steps toward having your Essential Conversations and developing your plan, you'll become more comfortable talking about your mortality and the mortality of those you love. And as you lean into the reality of mortality, you'll be amazed at how much more alive and awake you feel. Plus, you'll be better able to accept who you are and who other people are with more reasonable expectations and fewer resentments. And, you'll be able to take action based on what you discover to be true about yourself and others. We all have challenges, but you will become more patient with yourself and your loved ones. With the help of the Life Compass Plan Protocol we'll unpack in this chapter, you'll learn and grow as a person and experience more interdependence and mutual support in your relationships. Because of that, you'll experience the biggest payoff of all: creating a Shared Life Vision with the people you love that will allow you to live life more fully and with less unnecessary stress and chaos. So, let's look at how to have our Essential Conversations that will lead to the development of our Shared Life Visions that will produce your Life Compass Plan.

HAVING ESSENTIAL CONVERSATIONS THAT BUILD YOUR LIFE COMPASS PLAN AND SHARED LIFE VISION

It's my life's mission to spread the idea of creating a Life Compass Plan before any of life's unforeseen crises occur, what I call Life Quakes. Unfortunately, that's not how it always happens. Oftentimes, when people sit down to plan, it's because they're in the midst of a Life Quake … and that's OK. When you get through the crisis and meet the needs that are there, I encourage you to celebrate the fact that you have one another, that you got through it, and then identify what you've learned together from that experience and how you can incorporate those lessons into your lives. Meeting our basic needs together is always the place to start, even if it feels like an invasion caused by a Life Quake. Notice how meeting those needs while honoring one another's Life Compass not only equips you to flourish but gives you the precious experience of knowing you have People.

Whether you're in a Life Quake or, hopefully, creating a Life Compass Plan *before* a Life Quake, don't move forward without having your Essential Conversations. The Essential Conversations framework is made up of four stages: Discover. Determine. Define. Delegate.

Discover

The first stage is Discover. Here you will share with one another your Life Story, the Person part of your Life Compass. Do this in a way that makes it positive and fun and adventurous. Let one another know who you are, where your life is and where your life is going. If you and the individuals in your Family of Choice have already been introduced to Life Compass Living, this phase of the process will move more quickly. If you are introducing the Life Compass concept to your People, be

The creative ideas that emerge during your Essential Conversations are truly endless and inform your Life Compass Plans.

patient. Share what you're learning and spark their interest. Perhaps invite them to read this book and join you in a book discussion that unfolds over a two- to three-month period of time. Your goal during this phase is simply to discover one another's values and dreams for today and the future. Don't worry about having to be clear on everything. Work on being able to speak for yourself. And as you listen to others, work to truly understand and honor them without judgment.

Determine

The second stage is when you Determine the way you want to be in each other's lives. This is where you focus on the People and Place parts of the Life Compass. During this phase, you'll ask questions like these: Who would like to share a Life Compass journey? How will we help one another live in alignment with our Life Compass? How do we envision supporting one another when it's necessary? How do you define home right now? What will it mean to be at home in the future? If home in the future looks different, how will you know when it's time to move toward that Place? Will some of you choose to live together? If so, what will this look like?

Again, don't worry about walking away from one discussion with everything figured out. This phase is simply to Determine who wants to actively participate in the journey and what that journey may look like. This is a process that you'll continue to explore together. Eventually, your path together will become clear and produce the details of your Shared Life Vision and Life Compass Plan.

Define

Once you've discovered your Person and determined your People and Place, (your Shared Life Visions and a basic understanding of your Life Compass) the third stage of your Essential Conversations will involve defining the Life Compass roles you each will play in your Shared Life Vision. The roles you play will provide the emotional and practical support each person needs. In this stage, you'll ask one another questions like these: Will we create a financial fund that we'll all contribute to and share when there's a need? (Partners in a committed relationship do this most often, but you may expand the vision of how shared funds can be used to secure your present and future.) If so, who will oversee the fund? Do we want to share meals together? If so, is there someone who wants to oversee putting together a monthly meal plan? (Grandmothers could teach classes on this but we may lack the power of their influence and the culinary skills that draw participants.) Is there someone willing to do grocery shopping? (I remember going into my grandfather's garden for what was needed.) If living that intertwined on a practical level isn't what you envision or isn't possible because of distance, perhaps you look at ways to focus on supporting one another emotionally. Pick a day and time that you commit to having a check-in time, either in person, by phone, or even FaceTime or Zoom. (I regularly watch my grandchildren play in Scotland. I am grateful for technology!) The possibilities are endless as to how you define your vision and roles. There's no right or wrong way to share your life together. The point is to do it intentionally in shared responsibility.

Delegate

Lastly, you'll begin to Delegate the action steps of the Life Compass Plan that will ultimately fuel your Shared Life Vision moving forward. First, prioritize your action steps to ensure that anyone in a crisis has their needs met. I call these your Priority Actions. If there's no crisis, then begin what I call your Progressive Planning as you have your Essential Conversations and collect what you decide and plan to accomplish. Keep moving your next steps to the Priority Action List. Everyone can stay current on this short list in order to move forward together. At the end of the book I will show you how to use a form I developed to inform and direct your Essential Conversations as well as fully support your Priority Actions. Unless you are in a Life Quake, keep the Priority Actions in the flow of how you flourish. As my friend April says often, "We overestimate what we can do in a week and underestimate what we can do in a year."

Remember, your Life Compass Plan and Shared Life Vision are intended to support each individual's Life Compass. We are learning to flourish together, so we want to move together without unnecessary anxiety while building our Life Compass Plan. At this point, you'll need to collect what you Discover, Determine, Define, and Delegate, and do a periodic review to make whatever adjustments may be needed.

The Life Compass Plan you develop through your Essential Conversations will not only help you know where you want to collectively go together, but will also help you discover and direct the resources so that everyone can flourish in each stage of life. Remember, resources in the Life Compass Living Community are anything or anyone that meets a current or future need. There have been numerous examples of this with COVID-19. Families of Choice have rallied around one another to keep each other safe. I've known some folks who have either elderly individuals or individuals with underlying health conditions in their Circles of Connection. When the pandemic hit, they banded together to determine who would be the designated ones to go to the store and deliver food and supplies to those who need to remain in their homes. They've also determined how to help those who have lost income due to layoffs. Being able to depend on one another during this time has lessened the vulnerability caused by the pandemic.

The same goes for allocating resources to help make hopes a reality. I've seen folks plan to financially help one of their younger members go to a YMCA summer camp and another group that raised enough money between them to pay for tuition and books for one of their younger members to go to college. The creative ideas that emerge during your Essential Conversations are truly endless and inform your Life Compass Plans.

As you go through the planning process, keep these keys for progress in mind: *intention, Essential Conversations, time,* and *Parallel Planning.* You have to be intentional in creating the time and space for your own continuous self-discovery and the discovery of your people through your Essential Conversations. This is true, even if you are shaping a Shared Life Vision with someone who won't fully participate in the conversations. For instance, an aging parent who might not want to acknowledge that they will help with chores or make decisions. Or, a young adult who refuses to reflect on life, choose their relationships, and make good, solid choices that equip them for a healthy life and a secure future. Or, even a friend you care deeply about who is continuously making decisions that negatively impact their life. In these scenarios remember the idea of Parallel Planning that we discussed in Chapter 3. Be sure to leverage your people who are equally committed to your Life Compass Living journey and Shared Life Vision to help you come up with your Parallel Plan to manage how you share life with those people you love who aren't active participants. If you're experiencing anxiety about a certain person or situation, ask yourself where this person or situation exists in your Life Compass Plan. In this case, anxiety is your friend. It will always remind you that you need to intentionally take the time to either create or revisit a plan.

‹◇› PARALLEL PLANNING ‹◇›

A LIFE COMPASS PLAN IN ACTION

One example of forming a Life Compass Plan comes from a friend of mine, whose name is Jamie. Jamie spent five years talking to his life partner and parents (who are now in their late 70s) about creating a multigenerational home together. Jamie is a social worker and has seen firsthand how stressful it is to care for an aging parent. The four of them have had ongoing Essential Conversations about what they each want as they age, and his parents said early on that they'd rather live with one of their kids and have care brought in versus going to an assisted living environment. Truth be told, even if they wanted to go into an assisted living environment, they couldn't afford it. They also couldn't afford their current home *and* in-home care.

Knowing this and knowing that our health can change in a moment, especially as we reach our 70s, Jamie was ready for everyone to move in together when he was first introduced to the multigenerational concept. In his mind, it was a "no-brainer," and there were times that he was very frustrated that he was the "lone wolf" in their discussions. In his parents' minds, the thought of moving in with their adult child was completely overwhelming, scary, and sad on many levels. Accepting that we're aging and will eventually die is one of the hardest things any one of us ever has to face as a human being. In his partner's mind, the thought of having her in-laws with increasing care needs in her home felt smothering and not something she signed up for in the relationship.

Going through the Life Compass Protocol and changing their perspective of aging from being a "drag" to an "adventure" fast-tracked all four of them to the point that they have now combined their households. Prior to finding a house, they figured out whose names would be on the title, how much they would put down and what they needed from a "space" standpoint (his parents wanted their own kitchenette, bedroom, bathroom, and living area). And that's exactly what they found. A house with a full basement that includes a kitchenette, bedroom, bathroom, and living area. Jamie's parents now have the money they made from the sale of their home in an interest-bearing account and will use it for in-home care services if and when they are needed. If one of them has to have skilled nursing, they will use whatever money they have remaining to pay for that level of care until it runs out. They'll then start the Medicaid application process and access Medicaid funding. (Medicaid is a joint federal-state program in the United States that provides health coverage to certain categories of low-asset people, including children, pregnant women, parents of eligible children, people with disabilities, and the elderly needing nursing home care.)

> ⊕
> Breathe deep and make peace with reality. It is the only place to flourish that is not an illusion.

Since they are now paying less for their mortgage and living expenses, they've collectively freed up resources to address not only their basic needs but to also fund their individual and collective ideas of what it means to flourish. For example, they were able to afford a larger beach house for their family vacation this year, as well as contribute a few extra dollars to some people in their Outer Circles of Connection who they knew needed some financial help. These may seem like little things to some but, to them, they're significant.

Jamie and his family will continue to have their Essential Conversations framed around each person's Life Compass as they continue the journey together. They'll do the best they can to plan for each "expected" life transition, knowing full well that there's only so much they can control. They've talked about what happens if Jamie or his partner gets sick before one or both of his parents die, and they'll continue to openly discuss the potential realities, not with angst and anxiety but with an open mind and open heart, knowing they'll face whatever may be ahead together. The security they have gained relationally has been worth far more than any retirement account could ever provide.

I asked Jamie what was the biggest lesson he had learned so far going through the Life Compass Planning process. His response was one word: "patience." As we move forward, remember that each person you invite into your Essential Conversations can only be aware of what they're aware of, able to accept what they can accept, and ready to do what they are ready to do. Breathe deep and make peace with reality. It is the only place to flourish that is not an illusion.

HAVE YOUR ESSENTIAL CONVERSATIONS FROM THE INSIDE OUT

In order to better ensure that your Life Compass Plan fully supports you and your most important relationships, start your Essential Conversations from the inside out. What I mean by this is start having conversations with yourself and your spouse or life partner first. You (if you're single) and/or you and your partner (if you're in a committed relationship) are the center of your Circles of Connection and will want to direct how you participate together in your Family of Choice. This is often forgotten by those who neglect themselves in caregiving, chase goals that betray their Life Compass, or take those closest to them for granted. Take this seriously so you can avoid missing out on the life you want, burning out, or waking up in relationships that have dissolved due to neglect.

In Jamie's case, he and his partner had to be on the same page before they could make the move they did. Jamie deeply values his commitment to his family and his relationship with his parents. He also works a full-time job, loves to write music, and would like to vacation with his partner as often as he can. He considers his life partner and parents, his sister's family, and a few close friends to be his People (his Family of Choice). It's with these people that he feels at home. His Place is with them. This is Jamie's Life Compass.

Jamie's partner, Anne, also values family. However, she also values "space." Anne grew up with three brothers and her parents in a three-bedroom house with one bathroom. The minute she left home for college, she knew she never wanted to have that "crowded" feeling again. She also happens to be an extrovert and loves to spend time with a variety of people. Her calendar is often filled with dinners and bike rides with friends and, sometimes, a weekend trip here and there. Both of Anne's parents died when she was younger, so thinking about the needs of aging parents wasn't on her radar. However, saving for a retirement filled with travel has been. This is a high-level view of Anne's Life Compass.

Jamie is as much of an introvert as Anne is an extrovert. As the caregiving needs of Jamie's parents increased, so did Jamie's need to find time to be alone. The weight of the caregiving was bringing him down, and the demands of his work — combined with Anne's demands for him to engage in social activities — felt like he was being buried alive. The relationship was suffering, and neither Jamie nor Anne was flourishing.

As a social worker, Jamie knew that he would be the primary person in his family to help his parents navigate their medical resources. His sister is incredibly invested in helping their parents, too, but she has a teenager at home, two kids in college, a job that doesn't support her working remotely, and isn't as knowledgeable about the health care system. Both of his parents had already faced significant health issues, and both he and his sister had been incredibly stressed trying to tag team helping them in their current home. Knowing all of this, Jamie felt like it would be less time-consuming and easier on everyone if he and his parents lived at the same address. It would also be a financial win for everyone. His parents would have easy access to money for care (instead of it being tied up in the equity of their house), and he and his life partner would owe less on a mortgage plus would have more money available to invest in their future, since they'd be sharing living expenses with his parents.

Despite all of the seeming pros, there were also a few major cons. Anne couldn't imagine living with Jamie's parents. As a therapist who works with clients all day, the last thing she wanted was to "give up" her sacred space at home. Jamie was already inundated with their care. What would it be like if they lived together 24/7? Jamie's mother felt the same way. She and her husband loved their home. They had a master bedroom downstairs and enjoyed their own space. Not knowing what they would have to "give up" was scary. The push and pull between Jamie and Anne went on for at least three or more years.

Finally, one October, Jamie's dad needed emergency triple bypass surgery. It was then that everyone realized how overwhelming and expensive care needs can be in addition to maintaining two houses. This was the catalyst for the four of them to revisit their Essential Conversations and start looking at a Life Compass Plan that would include the four of them living under the same roof. They identified their non-negotiables and started the search for their combined Place. It was stressful at times, and none of them were exactly sure it was going to happen until, one day, "the" house came on the market. Because they had been planning, they were able to move forward very quickly. They found the house on March 16th, and Jamie and Anne sold their house and were moved in by May 1st. Jamie's parents followed on May 22nd, and sold their house a month and a half later.

Jamie's story is unique to Jamie and his family. I'm not suggesting that you follow their path. I'm simply using Jamie's story as an example of how to begin the planning process. *As you go through this process, focus on what clarity you have at the time and don't worry about the things that seem out of focus.* Jamie was clear on what he wanted years before his partner or parents. He didn't know exactly what he was looking for from a house standpoint, but he was clear that this is what he felt would be the best path forward. Through the Essential Conversations they've had over the years, the four of them have explored a variety of scenarios that included the option of his parents staying in their home with a reverse mortgage or even Jamie and his partner buying his parents' home and renting it back to them. They all had to be honest about what was clear for them at that moment in time. As they continued their conversations, the path they needed to take eventually became clear to all of them. However, the success they had was dependent on the reality that they began at the center of their Circles of Connection. Jamie and Anne had to be clear about what they needed first and foremost for their relationship. As did Jamie's parents.

As you begin your discussions, think about who it is that you, or you and your life partner, will show up for and who will show up for you. If you're married or in a committed relationship and something happens to you, will your partner continue to care for those people you have chosen and vice versa? There's no right or wrong answer. These are simply things that need to be pondered and discussed. For example, Anne has a disabled brother whom she spends a significant amount of time and money helping. In the event that Anne dies before Jamie, they've agreed that a certain amount of money from Anne's financial portfolio will be carved out to continue caring for her brother. Jamie will oversee the money, but her brother's son (Anne's nephew) will discern when it is needed. The same for Jamie's parents. If Jamie dies before Anne and his parents, the house will be paid for from his life insurance policy and a certain amount of money will be made available for any unexpected care needs that Jamie's parents may have. Anne will have access to the money, but Jamie's sister will be the one who determines when it's used and for what.

You'll also want to talk about advocacy. Who will you be an advocate for and who will be your advocate? We all need an advocate when we're in need, either because of the stage in life we're moving into or because of a Life Quake. As an advocate, you'll want to determine whether you'll be a "hands on" caregiver or an overseer of caregivers. You'll also want to think long and hard about whether you're willing to take on the responsibilities you believe may be "offered" to you as part of this role. You may be surprised to find that the people you assumed had a similar vision or definition of "caring" as you, don't. I've seen many people struggle with unspoken expectations they had from a sibling or a partner or a friend. *This* is why our Essential Conversations are so important. Life is too short to harbor resentments from unspoken expectations or miss dreams that could be possible. Stay true to your own Life Compass and that of the people closest to you.

GET DOWN TO THE BASICS FIRST

As you look at creating a Life Compass Plan for your own life and the lives of the people closest to you, start with a plan to meet your basic needs first. Basic needs can be viewed as those things necessary to maintain your physical life or enough safety and security to allow you to create relationships and stories beyond survival mode. If you're reading this book, you'll probably agree that the basic needs category also includes a larger list of practical and emotional support. I've seen people who are growing up and growing old with plenty to eat, a place to sleep, and health care who cannot find the motivation to keep going. They become discouraged and overwhelmed. It could be that what they *need* at a basic level is simply a friend. I could not be as content in my life as I wanted to be until I found a counselor and then found other Thought Partners who gave me the tools to build a life that was mine. We have to have enough *to live* and enough of other things *to want to live* before we can flourish in any significant way.

Tammy and I take stock regularly to ensure the basic needs of our relationship are met, and not just that we've divided up the chores. If we're going to have the relationship we want, there are some basic things we need to do and maintain. We *need* to have our date night. We *need* to protect our individual schedules to allow time for each one of us to maintain our spiritual practices to become mindful about how we live our lives and express our love of one another. That time was very difficult to protect with young children and all the demands of our roles in the world — parent, coach, employee, church member, friend, caregiver, etc. We discovered that when we treat these as optional luxuries, our love is displaced by survival instincts and consumeristic cravings. The price we pay when this happens reminds us that these things aren't "nice to haves." They're essential basic needs in the relationship and life we've chosen to invest in together.

One important thing to be aware of as you discuss your basic needs is that there will most likely be people in your Family of Choice who are in different income brackets. With that being said, someone in a lower income bracket may see basic needs as enough food, work, income, and transportation to not be in crisis each day. Whereas someone in a higher income bracket may define basic needs as enough food, work, income, transportation, a certain list of comforts, property, and privileges that come with having more resources. It's important to honor the fact that not everyone has the same definition of need or the same definition of flourishing. During your discussions, ask each other questions like these: Do people have what they need to live? Do they have what they need to support a healthy lifestyle? Do they have

> Together, we can help one another not only meet our basic physical needs but also the needs that make our souls dance.

what they need to get medical care? Do they have what they need to have medical assistance when they are unable to care for themselves? Do they have a place to live that is consistent, that can be maintained? Do they have a plan to flourish financially? What I mean by "flourish financially" isn't necessarily about some significant amount of money. I'm simply suggesting we help one another create a basic budget (if we don't already have one) and then progress to a budget that includes an emergency fund, then a savings account and then, if possible, to one that includes a financial plan, insurance, and investments so that we can not only secure our basic needs, but flourish now and into the future.

As we progress in our Essential Conversations, notice how we often-times purchase services that could be provided by people who care about and support us, which allows us to save our money for unexpected expenses or even making our dreams or the dreams of others come true. For example, following Jamie's dad's bypass surgery, Jamie's parents were spending $20 an hour to have a Certified Nursing Assistant (CNA) spend the night so that Jamie's mom could get some sleep. $20 an hour for 8 hours a night was adding up quickly, and the CNA was really only helping Jamie's dad walk to the bathroom during the night. Instead of continuing to spend that money, Jamie's nieces and nephews, who were home from college for Christmas break, were able to take nights and stay with their grand-father. Instead of paying $20 an hour, Jamie's mom paid them $10 an hour. This provided them some income for Christmas gifts and offered the opportunity for them to spend time with their grandfather during a very vulnerable time in his life. Also, Jamie's dad needed to go to the cardiologist for several appointments in a row following his surgery, and Jamie and his sister couldn't take any more time off work to take him. A retired friend from church was able to transport Jamie's dad to and from the appointments and provide updates to Jamie, his mom, and his sister. As I previously mentioned. I've seen Families of Choice come together not just to help with meals, transportation, a place to live, or help with medical care, but also to raise money to pay for tuition, books, summer camp, art classes, music lessons, a dream vacation, and more. Together, we can help one another not only meet our basic physical needs but also the needs that make our souls dance.

Before we move on to our future needs, there's one more basic need, and that's having our legal affairs in order. This includes all of the legal paperwork necessary to protect our resources, our property, our finances, our ability to live where we want to live, and to live as we want to live, the agreements that we have with other people (in our work and our businesses), and the ability to legally transfer property and finances in the best way possible. Stay tuned for the specifics of this in the next chapter. For now, I just want us to think about this as a basic need for anyone 18 and older, regardless of how much money we have in our bank account or how healthy we may be.

THEN LOOK TO WHAT YOU'LL NEED IN THE FUTURE

As soon as you have met the basic, current needs of your own life and those in your household, continue the same process with others in your Family of Choice. Once complete, begin to focus on the relationships and resources you'll dedicate to the future of your Shared Life Vision — and even the future of those who will live their lives long after you're gone. To do this, I suggest that each Life Compass Plan include the current life stage of each person and the next two life stages. A Shared Life Vision is not complete until it includes the next two life stages.

Some of the families I've worked with begin their Essential Conversations with their basic current needs met. They are not in crisis, but they are anticipating a number of Life Transitions for which they want to be better prepared. Typically, these folks have already gone through a Life Transition with a parent, other family member, or friend, and it's made them realize the need to plan for their future needs.

Remember, there are different vulnerabilities and different abilities in each stage of life. Where are you? Where are the people closest to you? Where are the people in your Family of Choice? What do you anticipate in the future? Do you have the resources and plans and understandings and agreements to dedicate to your future needs and to the next transitions that you'll be making? As you create a Shared Life Vision together, keep in mind that some relationships are for a season in life, and other relationships are for all of life. Some relationships will survive Life Transitions and Life Quakes, but others won't. Planning for future needs and creating a Shared Life Vision together will change with each person within a Family of Choice. How will you and the people you support deal with a health crisis? How will your lives adjust when someone dies, when someone is no longer part of the Family of Choice, which also can happen because of relocation and other reasons? What will happen if someone who's employed becomes unemployed? Are you in a place where you can save or have investments that hedge against the devastation that can happen when income changes? Do you have an emergency fund? And what do you need to do to generate income today to not only feed an emergency fund but also an account that accumulates wealth so that you can retire or even flourish during the Mutual Care and Dependent Care life stages? Will you have a separate account that you share with your Family of Choice that will be there in the event that someone loses their job or has unexpected medical bills? These are the types of questions we ask as we explore our future needs.

Notice how different it is to consider our future needs as we age versus the future needs of a baby about to be born. We tend to plan as a Family of Choice

A Shared Life Vision is not complete until it includes the next two life stages.

for a birth and avoid planning for the other Life Transitions that come later. We're not surprised and unprepared for a baby as often as we are the normal progressions that include no longer earning income and the death of someone significant in our lives. What if we were to plan for our future needs like we plan for the arrival of a new baby? Imagine having a plan for how we'll spend our days when we retire. Imagine knowing ahead of time that we have enough life insurance to cover the remaining balance of our mortgage in the event we die before our partner or vice versa. Imagine knowing the signs that we can no longer physically manage our home on our own and who we'll call when this happens. We plan for those coming into the world. Why not plan for the day we'll go out of this world, including the different stops that we know we'll pass along the way if we live long enough, like Mutual Care and Dependent Care? It was interesting for me to learn that 40% of the people on Medicare, the U.S. government health care plan, are under age 65. In other words, it's not just the progression of aging and life stages that brings people to the point of needing that kind of support. It could be any number of things. Car accident. Chronic illness. Stroke at an early age. Is it fun to think about these things? No, not necessarily at the time. But the gift we give one another in doing so is truly just as beautiful as the gift of a newborn. We remain worthy of love and care even after we stop being so cute and learn to talk.

In planning for future needs, I like to lean on the work of Dr. Amy, who happens to be a Life Transitions expert. (Remember, Life Transitions have many forms and Life Quakes are those Life Transitions that happen without notice and/or without a plan.) When Dr. Amy works with clients or speaks to audiences about Life Transitions, especially those that occur in midlife and beyond, she talks about a universal desire we all have — the ability to maintain choice, control, and independence in our lives forever. In order to do this, she suggests we engage in the 3 Ts: the things we need to *think about*, the things we need to *talk about*, and the things we need to *take action on*.

Admittedly, most of us don't know what we don't know, and we don't know where to begin. Dr. Amy recommends folks ask themselves this question: "If there were a shift in my health or mobility or the health or mobility of someone I love, what would I do differently in my relationships, activities, and where I live?" After spending time with thousands of people, Dr. Amy says this is the piece that most people miss when it comes to proactive planning. We certainly can't plan for *everything*, but we can plan for what Dr. Amy calls the *four implications* that accompany every Life Transition or every Life Quake. These include *practical* implications, *emotional* implications, *financial and legal* implications, and *family* implications. I like this framework as a planning tool because it breaks down the parts we need to focus on in a simple and straightforward way.

In the ongoing process of having our Essential Conversations and forming our Life Compass Plans, we will anticipate and respond to Life Transitions.

Life Transitions come in many forms. The ones I consider the most common and important to begin planning for include a health crisis, a job loss, a relationship change (such as a divorce, death of a spouse or relocation), retirement, and end of life.

Here is a list to use as you form your Shared Life Vision and Life Compass Plan. You will want to plan for what you can if any of these transitions occur in the lives of those you support as well as those who support you.

- Practical needs change
- Emotional needs change
- Life Compass changes
  - Person
  - People
  - Place
- Life Stage progression

- Life Quakes
- Financial resources change
- Professional support is needed or changes

To illustrate how planning ahead helps address the practical, emotional, financial/legal, and family implications of a transition, I've included the two scenarios below. As you read them, think of the transitions that have already occurred in your life and/or the lives of others and the ways in which you can either directly or indirectly relate to John, Susan, their kids, and John's mother.

A LIFE QUAKE WITH A LIFE COMPASS PLAN

John (55) and Susan (52) have been married for 30 years and have three grown kids, Noah (age 28), Ginny (age 25), and Joe (age 22). John works as a network operations director at a large for-profit company. Susan is a home stager and designer. All of the kids are living on their own. Noah is a physician's assistant, just got married last year, and is living about five hours away. Ginny is a paralegal, is in a relationship that will most likely lead to marriage, and lives in the same town. Joe is single and has just started a master's in business administration program at a university that's about seven hours away. Both of Susan's parents and John's dad are deceased. John's mother is in her late 70s and lives in her own apartment. She's had some challenges with neuropathy but is in overall good health.

Everyone in the family has pretty much enjoyed perfect health until about a year ago, when Susan started having severe headaches. At first, her primary care physician told her it was most likely tension-related and referred her to a local chiropractor and massage therapist. After a few months with no relief, she was sent for an MRI, which showed that she had a fast-growing brain tumor. The bottom line is she was told that, even if the tumor was surgically removed and she went through both chemo and radiation, she most likely wouldn't live more than six months. Obviously, the entire family was devastated.

Susan agreed to the surgery and reluctantly agreed to the chemo and radiation. Initially, she felt like it would make her too sick to have any quality of life in her remaining days, but John and the kids wanted her to give it a shot for them, so she did.

Fortunately, both John and Susan have good health insurance, and both had decided to get a cancer policy when they were in their 30s, since they watched what Susan's family went through when her mother was diagnosed with cancer. They've been having Essential Conversations with their kids, John's mother, and a few close friends they've known for years now and understand the importance of planning for transitions. The kids haven't wanted to think or talk about either of their parents or grandmother getting sick, much less dying, but as the discussions have continued, it's gotten easier for them to talk openly. Honestly, they thought it would be John's mother who would have a health crisis first, so despite all the planning and conversations, they still felt blindsided by Susan's diagnosis. Understandably so.

The two weeks that Susan was in the hospital were exhausting, but they kept in constant communication and worked as a team to ensure that no one person carried the brunt of the stress. Ginny took a few days off at the beginning to relieve her dad. She'd spend the night at the hospital while he slept at home and vice versa. John's mother took up cooking and keeping the dog. Noah took a few days off to relieve Ginny so she could go back to work. Joe came home for the surgery. Once the surgery was over and he was able to see Susan in the recovery room, he headed back for classes. Once she arrived home and started chemo, Joe came back and worked on his classes remotely. He was there to take her to chemo on the days that John needed to be in a meeting at the office. John and Susan's friends have also been contributing meals, doing laundry, and running other errands when needed.

Fortunately, Susan has been cancer-free for a year now. She's slowly gaining her strength back each day. The short-term disability policy she decided to get at the last minute has expired, but, after many long discussions, John's mother decided to move in with them and her rent is filling the gap of Susan's lost income. So, Susan's decided not to work for at least another six months to a year.

This past year and a half have been tough, but also eye-opening. Noah and his wife have since gotten pregnant, Ginny and her boyfriend have since gotten engaged, Joe is getting ready to graduate with his MBA, and John is planning to leave his corporate job and start flipping houses, which has always been a dream of his. None of them take Susan's time or anyone else's time for granted. The kids all have their Health Care Power of Attorney documents in place and have made sure their retirement and bank accounts have beneficiaries. They're also very intentional about planning annual family vacations. Ginny visits at least once a week and the boys have FaceTime calls with their parents and grandmother once a week.

John is keenly aware of the fragility of his wife's health and has been seeing a therapist to help him cope not only with the demands of working and caregiving, but the likelihood that he will one day be a widower. It's not been easy to face the reality, but he's found great strength both with his therapist and in a cancer support group for spouses. He and Susan both have all of their end-of-life documents in place and they practice leaving nothing left unsaid on a daily basis. John's mother has even been motivated to ensure all of her end-of-life documents are in place, and has even started talking about what she'd like to see happen for her care if she lives long enough to need it.

John and Susan and their family are far from perfect, but the strength of their love and commitment to openly facing the vulnerabilities of being human together allows them to flourish, even in the tough times.

A LIFE QUAKE WITH NO LIFE COMPASS PLAN

John (55) and Susan (52) have been married for 30 years and have three grown kids, Noah (age 28), Ginny (age 25), and Joe (age 22). John works as a network operations director at a large for-profit company. Susan is a home stager and designer. All of the kids are living on their own. Noah is a physician's assistant, just got married last year, and is living about five hours away. Ginny is a paralegal, is in a relationship that will most likely lead to marriage, and lives in the same town. Joe is single and has just started a master's in business administration program at a university that's about seven hours away. Both of Susan's parents and John's dad are deceased. John's mother is in her late 70s and lives in her own apartment. She's had some challenges with neuropathy but is overall in good health.

Everyone in the family has pretty much enjoyed perfect health until about a year ago, when Susan started having severe headaches. At first, her primary care physician told her it was most likely tension-related and referred her to a local chiropractor and massage therapist. After a few months with no relief, she was sent for an MRI which showed that she had a fast-growing brain tumor. The bottom line is she was told that, even if the tumor was surgically removed and she went through both chemo and radiation, she most likely wouldn't live more than six months. Obviously, the entire family was devastated.

Susan agreed to the surgery, chemo, and radiation without question. There was no way she wouldn't take whatever possible medical interventions there were, even if they made her remaining time here on Earth miserable.

Fortunately, John and Susan have good health insurance. Unfortunately, their co-pays for the surgery, hospitalization, chemo, and radiation will most likely bankrupt them. They had discussed getting cancer policies in their 30s, after Susan's mother died, but neither of them wanted to pay the $38 a month when they were first starting their family. Plus, Susan never wanted to talk about either of her parents' deaths or even entertain the thought that she'd ever get cancer.

The two weeks that Susan was in the hospital were exhausting, and Ginny resents both of her brothers for placing most of the burden of being there on her. Even though her boss was understanding at the time, he's since been throwing the fact that she was gone for two weeks in her face. When she wasn't at the hospital, it was primarily Ginny and her grandmother who did the cooking and cleaning. Her dad was just too overwhelmed and sad. All he did was look out the window during the day and then go to the local bar at night. Some of their family friends came around in the beginning but, as time went on, they all went back to their own lives.

Fortunately, Susan has been cancer-free for a year now. She's slowly gaining her strength back each day, but she's going to have to go back to work or they're going to lose the house. John is still working, but Susan had no short-term disability and they've completely eaten through their savings. John's mother tries to help out, but she barely has enough money to pay her own rent much less contribute to helping them financially.

This past year and a half have been tough. Noah and his wife have since gotten pregnant and Noah has increased his work hours, so he's hardly ever home. Ginny and her boyfriend split up over Ginny's angry outbursts and never being available for him. Joe had to extend his MBA program another year due to missing classes because of partying too much. And John is still working the same job. He'd give anything to follow his dream of flipping houses, but now they're in so much debt he feels like he'll never be able to retire. They all got together at Christmas and, every now and then, the boys will call and talk to Susan, but the rift between Ginny and the boys is still there. John's mother stops by when her friend can bring her, but it's not that often, and John and Susan rarely go see her. John's exhausted and continuing to drink in the evenings and weekends, and Susan doesn't feel up to visiting.

There's a heaviness in the house, and everyone feels it, yet no one wants to talk about it. Things were once "great." Now, they all walk around with a far-away look in their eyes.

Can you tell the difference between the energy in the two scenarios? Notice what we can control and what we cannot. John, Susan, the kids, and their mother weren't any less sad or scared about Susan's diagnosis in the first scenario, but they were definitely more prepared and comfortable talking openly with one another about difficult topics. This in turn helped them communicate better as a team, which reduced their stress levels, enabling them to make wiser choices in their responses and reactions to the reality they were all facing. Their Essential Conversations and planning empowered them to deal with the Life Quake of Susan's unexpected diagnosis with dignity, honor, and respect for themselves and one another. Yes, there were tears and sleepless nights, but none of them moved into self-harming behaviors like overworking and drinking to numb their pain. And, whereas they certainly had medical expenses, the amount was far from what they could have been had Susan not taken out a cancer policy and decided to invest in short-term disability as a contractor.

PLANNING SUMMARY

Now that we've explored how to have our Essential Conversations and progress through the planning process, it's time to move on to what needs to be done to protect what we're creating. Before we leave this chapter, though, let's recap what we've discussed.

First, we identified three big payoffs you'll experience by engaging in Essential Conversations and building a Life Compass Plan with your People. 1. You'll become more secure. 2. Your relationships will become more intentional and secure. 3. You'll make progress on the Trajectory of Readiness — the ability to accept life and be present and participate in it as it is — not how we want it to be or hoped it would be but more as it is.

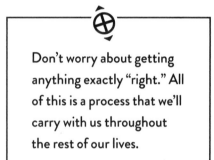

Don't worry about getting anything exactly "right." All of this is a process that we'll carry with us throughout the rest of our lives.

Next, we talked about the importance of creating a Life Compass Plan before life's unforeseen crises occur, what I call Life Quakes. Then, we dove into the four phases of the Essential Conversations framework: Discover. Determine. Define. Delegate.

Finally, we explored the need to plan for the basic needs of yourself and your household first, and then expand to planning for the basic needs of others in your Family of Choice. Then, begin the process of planning for your future together. Don't forget to include the current life stage of each person and the next two life stages.

There's a lot of material here, so I recommend reading this chapter a few times. And, whatever you do, don't worry about getting *anything* exactly "right." All of this is a process that we'll carry with us throughout the rest of our lives. There are many things we have power and control over and many things we don't. The better we get at knowing the difference between the two, the more peace we'll have.

On to Protection we go.

CHAPTER 6

Protection

*"Not everything that is faced can be changed; but
nothing can be changed until it is faced."*
— James Baldwin

*"As for the future, your task is not to foresee it, but
to enable it."* — Antoine de Saint-Exupéry

When you think of protecting someone or something, what comes to your mind? I think of deadbolt locks, a security system, or any number of weapons that can be used to keep myself and those I love safe. And I'm not an aggressive kind of guy. In fact, I'm definitely more about peace than I am war. But when it comes to someone I love suffering, I can become a warrior.

In this chapter, I am not wanting to supply the knowledge and information available from professionals and those who have published wisdom and detailed considerations in these areas. I simply want to get you started and/or encourage you to follow through on a very important list.

As we begin our adventure together, we need to first and foremost ensure that we protect the dignity and resources of ourselves and our loved ones. To do this, there are a few Priority Actions that we need to take. For many of us, these actions can seem confusing and overwhelming, so it can be tempting to bury our heads in the sand and ignore them. But if we're really serious about flourishing in every stage of life — and our eventual death — it's absolutely critical that we get these done. Knowing that you're prepared for the far-too-common situations and crises we face as aging mortals will make every ounce of energy you put into this worth it. In fact, I guarantee you will experience a real and substantial payoff, both practically and emotionally. Best of all, you'll discover the gift of identifying the people you trust the most, the ones who will be there for you in the toughest moments.

To make these tasks as simple as possible, I've created what I call the First Folder Checklist. **Every task on the First Folder Checklist is needed by every adult where there is a legal system and private property.** This bolded sentence isn't intended to scare you. It is, however, intended to get your attention. I can't emphasize enough its importance. Even if you don't do everything we overview in this chapter, *any progress you make will be worth celebrating.* This will get you moving toward membership in the elite group of people who have additional protections for themselves, and will have given priceless gifts to those they love, should they be needed.

⊕ **first**folder

Dying is a fact of the human journey, and yet our culture does very little to embrace that fact. As a result, we miss out on the precious gift found in our dying. In his notebooks, Albert Camus said, "Come to terms with death. Thereafter, anything is possible." We have limited time to build a shared future together. The terror around dying and the denial encouraged by our consumer culture, and what Stephen Jenkinson calls the "death trade," can cause many pathologies and foolish decisions.[10] As we're able to come to terms with the common frailty of being human and our eventual death, we're better able to make decisions about how to live. The primary purpose of Life Compass Living is to help us stop denying that life is limited, messy, and tenuous, and learn how to design our lives to be more expansive, compassionate, intentional, and secure.

Please note: As we move into the First Folder Checklist, it's important for me to state that I am not an attorney and I'm not a financial advisor, nor do I pretend to be. What I'm sharing with you is what I've learned through trial and error for myself and while working with others in the United States. If you can afford to meet with an attorney and financial advisor, I strongly urge you to do so. A good estate attorney should be able to provide you with a Care Plan that walks you through long-term care planning for yourself and/or another loved one, especially throughout the mutual and dependent care stages. Remember, it's best to be thinking at least two Life Stages ahead. If you can't afford an attorney or financial advisor, you can still protect your family, with or without either professional. Don't let that stop you. However, consider talking with your Core Relationships about sharing the expense together. It's information that's well worth the investment, especially if it can be shared by many.

> As we're able to come to terms with the common frailty of being human and our eventual death, we're better able to make decisions about how to live.

THE FIRST FOLDER CHECKLIST

Item #1: Prepare Your Last Will and Testament

A last will and testament is a legal document that communicates a person's final wishes pertaining to possessions and dependents. It is a legal document that needs to be done correctly and one of the major factors that shape our legacies. If you are an adult and do not have a will, or your will has become stale (not expressive of your current life stage or desires), now is the time to move forward on this. If you have a will that is current, good for you! I encourage you to share this fact with your closest friends and family. You never know who it may motivate to get this incredibly important task done. Believe me when I say, they and their loved ones will thank you.

You will want to know how probate works where you live. Probate is a legal process that takes place after someone dies. It includes: proving to the appropriate legal body that a deceased person's will is valid (usually a routine matter if the deceased was prepared), identifying and inventorying the deceased person's property, paying all commitments and debts, and then distributing the remaining property as state law directs (since there's no will). This can be an expensive and time-consuming process for your family members. If you don't put a will of your own making in place, one will be provided for you as part of probate. I will repeat this along the way, but using an attorney is helpful because the legal process can only produce the results you want when you put the appropriate legal documents in place to communicate your wishes and empower the people needed to carry that out. My hope here is simply to help you engage in this important task so you can avoid the perils and expenses of dying without a will (intestate).

Remember, our lives transition through Life Stages, and those transitions can often be tricky to navigate. We grow into work and career, and family. We transition into the second half of life and learn to embrace the process of aging. The importance of a will may be found at any point, in any stage, and everyone who is impacted by our death will be helped by completing this task.

At our death, all of our property will be released from our control. In fact, everything that is ours to control, and even those things that we have partial control over, will be released after we've died. I have seen many relatives and friends sort through the possessions of parents after their deaths. The houses were often littered with everything they used and stowed. There were decades of possessions on display and tightly tucked away. It was overwhelming to those who had to go through it all! And this was just what was in the house. They also had to clean up all of the administrative and legal aspects of the other property, money, and businesses, which is an incredibly overwhelming process. People have commented that funeral processions don't include a U-Haul. One woman, when reflecting on her family's chaos after her mother died without a will in place, said, "Mom's up in heaven, but all hell is breaking loose down here." It doesn't have to be this way.

Are you the parent of a minor child? If so, "Who will parent your children?" is one of the most important issues that surface when we talk about a will and how it will direct all the resources we leave behind. Parents desire to be loving and caring, and provide well for their children. Please decide who will parent your minor children if you can't, and add a last will and testament to the list of **basic things** you need to have in place. Include in your plans how your child(ren) will be supported, and com-

> The importance of a will may be found at any point, in any stage, and everyone who is impacted by our death will be helped by completing this task.

municate your priorities in raising your children to those people who will parent them. You'll also want to make sure any resources you have can flow smoothly and in a timely manner toward their care. Make sure you discuss your plans with those you've designated to care for your minor children. Show them where to find the things they'll need to have if your unforeseen death were to happen. I know this may sound morbid, but some people have said that securing people in this role gave them a peace that surprised them and a deep gratitude for those willing to accept the role. Your children will be under a tremendous amount of angst and grief if, God forbid, you were to unexpectedly die or get sick with a terminal illness. The last thing they need is for adults to be arguing over what needs to happen next. Please do the work of finding the security and strength within yourself to stop delaying this necessary task if you have minor children. They are depending on you. I know our culture likes consumers who chase the lies of the independent self and permanence I introduced in Chapter 1. We can do better.

If you don't have your minor children in a will, the government will have a legal process by which they are entrusted to someone else. I've seen major disagreements and huge conflict in families where there was no designation of the people who would raise minor children upon the death of their parents. The stories are horrendous, and it is our duty as parents of minor children to make sure we have a last will and testament in place that directs their care if the labor and joys of providing that ourselves comes to an end.

I knew a man who had a farm and a family. His family shared many rich times together, and they had great affection for one another. His wife died, and then he died. After he died, the reality of what was left caused his family to be in great distress and conflict. The good news is they eventually worked through it. During one of our coaching sessions, one of the adult children said, "I hope we're still talking when this is over." I knew the father who had passed fairly well, and I knew he would not have wanted to see his children go through such conflict and spend so much of his hard-earned money working through the legal battles and decisions that had to be made. They all paid the price of him not having a current will.

So, first, remember dependent children. Make them the priority. Secondly, remember that everything you control, everything that's yours will be moving on after you die. In your last will and testament, you can direct how your possessions will be used, how they will be sold, and what happens to the money that is yours. It is on the checklist because it's something that every human will need. The other tasks on the checklist are needed by most of us, but some will be avoided by a sudden death. You know what they say about death and taxes. When you die (and you will), someone will pay any taxes due. Your will and an estate plan can make that bill smaller and cause those who pay the bill to be grateful to you for helping them do what will be necessary.

Every adult needs a will.

There are many resources that can help you put a last will and testament in place. As I previously mentioned, if you can afford it, I strongly suggest you use a licensed attorney in your state or province as you put a will together. Not only does that allow you to ask the attorney questions and find out what you need to know, but it also gives the attorney the ability to ask you questions. As you make clear what you want to accomplish with your will, the attorney can ensure you do it in the best way possible and in harmony with the laws that pertain to where you live. Some employers offer legal services as part of their benefit package. Don't forget to check this avenue when considering an attorney. Even if you don't use an attorney, make sure that you put a last will and testament in place that meets all the legal requirements in the jurisdiction where you live. There are internet sites that can guide you through the process.

Last but not least, It's important to know that "beneficiaries trump a will." What I mean by that is make sure the beneficiaries listed in your will match the beneficiaries you've listed on your accounts and that you keep both current. In court, a beneficiary listed on an account will override anything you've written in your will. This is a good rule of thumb to remember and is often missed and/or misunderstood.

Again, my goal here is simply for you to commit to putting a last will and testament in place. You'll either have a will of your own making or one prepared by the government officials where you live. My sincere hope is that you'll choose the former rather than the latter.

Item #2: Designate Beneficiaries

Here is a good place to start as you prepare, review, or update your last will and testament. Make sure every single one of your financial accounts has a current beneficiary listed. Retirement accounts. Bank accounts. Any and all accounts or insurance policies where you have money in your name. If you co-own an account with another person, you may want to identify more than yourselves on the beneficiary list. Contact the appropriate people today and start the paperwork necessary to make these beneficiary additions or modifications.

I remember when I learned that I could be listed as Payable Upon Death (POD) on my dad's bank account. It was as easy as going to the bank with my dad and having them make the simple changes. This change ensures that, upon your death, your cash will not be frozen and have to go through probate.

A friend of mine in her 40s was recently planning a trip out of the country with her partner. She made it a priority to go down to the bank and ensure her mother was the POD for her accounts in the event that she and her partner died on the trip. I don't know too many 40-year-olds who would have thought of that. Be wise at every age.

Advance Directives

As we work through our First Folder Checklist, we now move to advance directives. Your last will and testament is about what happens to your possessions and your dependents after you die. Advance directives (Medical POA and a Living Will) are about empowering someone to make decisions and speak on your behalf in the event that you can't do so for yourself. Having advance directives in place can help reduce unnecessary suffering for yourself and your loved ones when you're sick. They also will minimize the chaos that can invade some of the most vulnerable and anxiety-ridden moments of our lives.

Advance directives are about empowering someone to make decisions and speak on your behalf in the event that you can't do so for yourself.

Item #3: Medical Power of Attorney — Power of Attorney for Personal Care — Health Care Power of Attorney.

The first advance directive is a medical power of attorney or a power of attorney for personal care. It can also be referred to as a health care power of attorney (HPOA). You need to have a medical POA in place because there may be times when medical decisions need to be made for you and you are simply not able to make them.

A medical POA gives the person you choose the legal authority to direct your care in a way that's in harmony with what you want. They need authority and knowledge. It's not necessarily true that the people who love you most *know* what you want in terms of medical care unless you've actually discussed it with them. I've sat with weeping people who weren't certain what the best choice was for their family member's medical care: choosing between waiting to have surgery and having surgery; choosing between one medication or another; monitoring side effects and the prognosis that unfolds with each direction and treatment. These decisions can be hard enough when you're clear about what someone wants. So don't add to the distress of your loved ones by not empowering a medical power of attorney, and telling them how you would like your care directed.

Without a medical POA, physicians will do whatever they can for you, but it's important to realize that the care you need may have to be delayed while the physicians in charge make sure they have the correct authorization. They must protect themselves legally, and they want to do their best to know and honor the wishes of their patient.

Here are the two key things you'll want to discuss and document with your chosen medical POA:

1. Your current medical history and the names and phone numbers of others you trust who may have important information about your health that the medical power of attorney isn't aware of. This will enable everyone to more fully support you and your care.

2. The power to carry out your wishes when you die in regards to the disposition of your body and any funeral or memorial gathering. This is sometimes called the designation of agent for body disposition. Please check to make sure it is supported by the laws where you live. This can be accomplished with the help of a funeral home. Share this information with all who would be involved in carrying out your wishes so they will take direction from the appropriate person.

I have a friend who has written an actual checklist of items her designated medical POA is to do upon her death. The list is very detailed. For example, she has directed that if she's wearing her jewelry and she's in a hospital, to please have the nursing staff remove it and give it to her family. She also has decided to donate her body to science. Upon her death, she has directed her medical power of attorney to notify the organization to come pick her up. When the research is complete, her body will be cremated and her remains will be sent back to her family.

I'm not suggesting that you create a detailed checklist unless that's what you want to do. My hope is simply that, if you don't have a health care power of attorney in place, you'll at least begin thinking about these two things: what type of care you would want in the event that you need someone to represent you (i.e. you're unconscious and/or on a breathing tube) and who is the person or people who could serve in this very important role. Then, add it to your Priority Action List to begin these discussions. Also, if you have a child who's 18 years old, please have this discussion with him or her. A birthday gift for an 18th birthday could be a medical POA. It will create an adult conversation and you can avoid the real but rare possibility of being a parent with a child on a ventilator without the power to make a medical decision for him or her simply because they're now an adult and put this off. I don't like to use fear or guilt as motivators as we take on the work of Life Compass Living. Focus on the gift you are giving yourself and those who will be with you if this document is needed. Some wisdom blossoms slowly. This wisdom invites immediate action.

Item #4 Living Will

The next item on the First Folder Checklist is a living will. It's also called a declaration of a desire to die a natural death. I believe the decisions that are made in harmony with your living will are some of the most important in terms of maintaining your dignity during the times when you are the most vulnerable. I saw a woman return to a normal life after several months of her family preparing for her death. She had huge gratitude for how her living will was honored by her medical POA and the rest of the family and friends who came around her in those days. Some of us will die suddenly, with no decisions that need to be made. In that case, our last will and testament would take effect. We put a living will in place to maintain our dignity and reduce our suffering in the event our dying takes place over time.

If you become terminally ill or injured, what do you want to be done in order to extend your life? In the living will, you express in writing what measures you want taken for you in this case. It's not only important for you in order to maintain your dignity and have the care you want, it's vitally important to those who care about you, to those who will be present, to those who will be surrounding the person you've made your health care power of attorney. They will be making decisions about life and death, and it is good for you to give them the gift of clarity. It is good for you to empower them to know the decisions that you would make. As part of their path to peace, they can have the knowledge that they've done what you wanted.

Would you want your life extended by being hooked up to a respirator or a heart bypass machine? Would you want to have a feeding tube or to be fed intravenously? Would you want to be given medications that support a longer life but don't increase the likelihood that you would survive? These are among the decisions that are yours to make if you have a living will. And if you don't, they are among the decisions you are giving to your physician, guided by the people they can gather to help make those important decisions.

Let me share two stories. The first is from a person I know who is a surgeon. He's also on a hospital's ethics committee. He told me of a case where a woman was admitted to the hospital and had a health condition that had a sudden onset. Her diagnosis: if she was put on heart and lung bypass, she had a good chance to recover. But unless she was put on the bypass, she would not survive. Her son showed up in the hospital and insisted that his mother did not desire to be hooked up to any machine at any point. He argued forcefully that this was against his mother's wishes.

He did not have a health care power of attorney, but he was the closest relative present when a decision needed to be made.

The decision was made to put her on the heart and lung bypass and allow more time for a final decision to be made, since it was a weekend and they couldn't contact the other siblings. In just a matter of 24 hours, she began to improve and was taken off the life support system. When she gained consciousness and she was told what her son had said, she informed the physician that that was not true, that she would have wanted done what actually was done. She went on to share that her son had had a long history of addiction and had recently stolen several items from their house and sold them to buy drugs. She had informed him that she was going to take him out of her will until he was able to sustain sobriety. He needed his mom to die in order to receive his part of his inheritance. People in active addiction can die of their addiction when they are given large amounts of money from an estate or any other source. This young man may have survived the influx of money but his mother did not want to fund the direction his life was going and she wanted to have the medical support to continue living. This worked out well, but some do not.

In addition to demonstrating the need for a living will, this story points out the importance of the last will and testament that expresses your current wishes. It also points out the importance of having a health care power of attorney in place. All three were part of that story.

The second is my own mother's story. My mom was diagnosed with advanced non-Hodgkin's lymphoma. I told some of that story in the Preface. The treatment they used was an experimental protocol. It included a bone marrow transplant. While she was going through the bone marrow transplant, she contracted an infection and ended up in ICU. My mom had a living will. I was her medical power of attorney. She had made it clear to me, and in her living will, that she did not want to be hooked up to any machines. That was not in harmony with what I might've chosen, at least not in the context of a bone marrow transplant, but she had been clear with everyone, including my father.

On the night she died, I was in a hotel near the hospital. I received a call at 2 a.m. telling me that my mom had taken a turn for the worse, and I would want to come be with her. When I walked through the door of her room, she had coded. Her heart had stopped, and they were beginning to do CPR. They looked at me and asked, "What do you want us to do?"

I said, "Stop."

They replied, "Are you sure?"

"Yes," I clearly stated, and they stopped.

I cannot emphasize enough how much of a gift it was for my mother to have made her wishes known to me and my dad, and to the other people close to her. It was one of the hardest decisions I've ever had to make. It's a decision that I have second-guessed many times, but I can always come back to the reality that she had her living will in place. She communicated clearly what she desired to me, to my dad, and to my children. So, I continue to receive the support of the people around me when I second-guess myself. We did what she wanted. I was the one in the room who made the decision. It was what she wanted. My mom had a way of putting it when she would tell me or anyone else. She said, "If I die, you just let me go. Do whatever you need to deal with my leaving. But when it's my time, I want to go. I don't want to be like Lazarus and have to die twice."

There are many helpful tools online for thinking through the issues related to your living will. One of the best I've found that I point people to constantly are the *Go Wish* cards, developed by a group called Coda. You can find them online at coda.org. The *Go Wish* cards are 35 playing cards that have a list of things you would want to consider when putting together your living will and having those conversations with the person who has your health care power of attorney and the others who are close to you.

The way they suggest you use the cards is to look through the 35 cards and place them in three stacks. One stack represents the 10 most important things that you would want done if you were at the end of life. The second stack represents a list of things that are important, but not the most important. Then, the third stack are items not important to you at all.

Here are a few examples: one is having your financial affairs in order. Is that really important for you at the end of your life? To take care of unfinished business with family and friends? To have my funeral arrangements made? Those are among the things that you could take care of before you were terminally ill. But there are others. Having human touch. I know some people who want to have someone holding their hand or wiping a cold cloth across their forehead. Is that important to you? Another is to die at home. Some people want to die in the house, with the scenery, people, and smells of home. They want to be in their room, in their bed. Others want to be where the best care is given. Others don't believe the location is important at all.

What's important to you? I know some people want to have a crowd around when they're struggling. I know others who wish to be alone or only have specific people present. Some people pledge to never let a loved one be alone and go to great lengths to keep that pledge. I've seen families work diligently to maintain someone on watch. Is that something you would want done?

For some people, their biggest fear is not about what is beyond dying but the pain that may be part of the process of dying. The good news is that palliative care can do a lot to manage pain and anxiety at the end of life. But is the avoidance of pain most important to you? Another matter of importance for some is mental awareness. Some people's highest priority is to be able to consciously participate in the decisions being made or in the moments they have with loved ones. They would rather endure some pain in order to be able to know that people are around or to communicate with people.

Many individuals' greatest end-of-life desire is not being connected to machines. That was important to my mother. She believed she was in the care of God and that people were taking over when machines took over. But, that's not the desire of everyone, including me, her son. Being hooked up to machines can carry us through transitions. In connection to your living will, would you want machines to keep you alive?

Another important consideration is the maintenance of dignity. What would that mean? For some people, it would mean cleanliness and being covered, among other factors. This is when you can help those who will be caring for you and directing your care to know your priorities. So, if those things are important to you to maintain your dignity, it's important for you to help people understand what you want.

I found two of the cards extremely important. One was centered around having an advocate who knew my values and priorities. Of course, that points to having a health care power of attorney, but I also want to point out the word *advocate*. One of the most important things people need when they're receiving health care, and especially when they can't fully participate in decision-making themselves, is to have a well-informed advocate that is empowered to make decisions that need to be made. I think it's one of the most important things for me, having an advocate who knows my values and priorities. The health care providers and the systems that approve and pay for health care often need to be engaged by someone who is informed, empowered, and assertive. That is one reason we are addressing the First Folder Checklist inside our Essential Conversations. The more people who are informed, empowered, and assertive, the better.

The second most important card to me is the Wild Card. When I first saw it, I kind of chuckled and wondered what that was. I thought maybe it was a way the company protected itself for what might not have been included. Then, when I did the work myself, when I built my list, when I had my three stacks of cards, the Wild Card ended up in the list of the 10 most important.

My Wild Card would be essential! One of the things that would be most important for me at the end of my life is to have my music around. Whether it was recorded music or live music, I would want there to be music any time we weren't having conversation, any time we didn't need silence. Certainly, there will be moments when silence is appropriate. My wife, sons, and extended family will know what to do. They can pick up my Spotify and pick from the playlists that are there. But even without Spotify and a playlist, they would know my music. I would want to be going out to the songs that were part of my living. I'm sure the folks in my life would be singing along to many of those songs and having all the memories tied to the events that had those songs as the soundtrack. Put on some John Denver, Neil Young, Rush, Bach, Creedence Clearwater Revival, Larry Norman, B.J. Thomas, James Taylor — and that is just a few of the artists from my earlier years. Jason Isbell, Gretta Van Fleet, the Avette Brothers, and the Wood Brothers are supplying the melodies and moods of the days now. I think I want to go out with two songs from my favorite songwriters. They were written by my sons. I'll want Steven Fuller's song "If No Other" to be played loudly. Then crank up Tripp Fuller's song "Found You." In fact, if we're listening to a good one, I'll try to let us all finish singing the final chorus before I interrupt the moment with my exit.

A living will is there not only to inform medical professionals that need to be informed. It is there to help people know what you want in this immensely important moment when you're facing death. Because when we do death well, when we are with each other in the way we want to be with each other, it can be part of a great legacy and can make a huge difference in how those relationships go moving forward.

I also want to bring your attention to The Conversation Project (the-conversationproject.org). It's a good place to go to be guided through the process of putting together a living will. Another is The Death Café Movement. That is a gathering where people sit together in a safe place with tea or some snacks and talk about dying. It may not be something that sounds attractive to you, but I've gone to some Death Café gatherings and had some incredibly rich times with strangers. Dealing with our mortality is important, as we've stated before. So, putting together your advanced directives will not only ensure your ability to be supported the way you want in terms of health decisions, directing your property, and in terms of how you wish to be cared for and supported at the point of death, I believe it will also cause you and your people to sit and reflect in ways that will help you all make better choices about how you live.

> When we do death well, when we are with each other in the way we want to be with each other, it can be part of a great legacy and can make a huge difference in how those relationships go moving forward.

Item #5: Additional Power of Attorney Options — Property and Finances

The next item in the First Folder Checklist is the use of other types of POA. There are many ways to use a power of attorney related to your property and finances. Any time we need someone else to act on our behalf as a legal representative, we can use a POA. Some are only given to people for a specific task. Others are broader in their scope. Some are for a specific time, and others remain in place until a specific date or event, or our death. Here is a list to consider:

- **General Power of Attorney.** In this situation, the agent can perform almost any act as the principal, such as opening financial accounts and managing personal finances. A general power of attorney arrangement is terminated when the principal becomes incapacitated, revokes the power of attorney or passes away.

- **Durable Power of Attorney.** This arrangement designates another person to act on the principal's behalf and includes a durable clause that maintains the power of attorney after the principal becomes incapacitated but ends when the principal dies.

- **Special or Limited Power of Attorney.** In this instance, the agent has specific powers limited to a certain area. An example is a power of attorney that grants the agent authority to sell a home or other piece of real estate.

- **Springing Durable Power of Attorney.** In some jurisdictions, a "springing" power of attorney is available and becomes effective when a specified event occurs, such as when the principal becomes incapacitated.

My father gave me a limited POA to settle issues with his car when he was not able to do so. Once I had sold the car and deposited the money, the POA was void.

I also had a durable POA that gave me control over his property and finances. I followed his direction when he could make the decisions. I was also able to make decisions when his dementia progressed and he could not. You want to put this in place when you are of sound mind so there is no disputing among family that this is indeed what you wanted.

The key issue is the protection of and the continued work of all your property and finances when you are unable to make decisions yourself. This will make it possible for bills to get paid, business transactions to continue, and for you to know that everyone who depends on the management of your assets will stay current until you are able to take on that role again. You can decide if you want this to be "durable." A durable power of attorney does indeed give the person you designate the ability to direct your property or finances. You can be specific as to what areas you wish to give them the power of attorney over. This may be used for a short period of time when you're recovering from an illness or from a surgery and you are either unable or simply don't wish to give full consideration to these decisions. I've seen people who had a sudden illness or accident who spent a great deal of time unable to direct their financial affairs. Some recovered and others did not. The ones without a power of attorney in place caused unnecessary hardships on the people they supported, and their businesses suffered as well.

You can also choose to do the "springing" power of attorney. This simply means that your power of attorney will "spring" into effect if you are deemed incapacitated by a physician. The primary difference between the two is that a durable power of attorney becomes effective as soon as you sign the document and remains in effect if you are incapacitated. The springing power of attorney goes into effect only if you are deemed incapacitated.

Again, there are two important elements in setting up a durable power of attorney. One is to make sure it's done in harmony with the laws where you live. This is, again, why I suggest using an attorney, although there are durable power of attorney forms available online. Secondly, you need to have conversations with whomever is assigned the power of attorney so they will know in detail what you would want done in any case where the power of attorney would be used.

The person or persons given a POA of any kind will need to have access to current information related to the property and finances they will control. Be mindful about whether your state or province requires that you register your power of attorney with your county's Register of Deeds or other government office. I've learned from some that they were directed to file a power of attorney at the courthouse when it wasn't necessary to do so. Having this type of information made public when it doesn't need to be can put people, especially seniors, at risk. Unfortunately, we live in a world where elder abuse is rampant and there are criminals who prey on those who are vulnerable. These types of documents have names, addresses, and more. Just double-check. It's better to be safe than sorry.

I can imagine some people thinking that a durable power of attorney is something that's only for the wealthy. However, in the end, my father's estate was worth $2,002. But even during the last couple of years of his life, I used the durable power of attorney on many occasions. This might be considered by many to be meager finances, but every dollar was very important in terms of the quality of his care and his ability to continue supporting the people and the charities that he desired to support. He had monthly income that ceased at his death but needed to be managed responsibly.

My dad had already made me his power of attorney for property when his dementia began to progress. On a couple of occasions, it was that power of attorney that enabled me to stop some financial agreements he made when he was not able to fully understand the commitment he was making. I had some heated conversations with people who were taking advantage of my father's mental state. Because I had the power of attorney, and I could produce copies of it, I was able to free my father from commitments he would not have made if he'd had full use of his mental capacities.

If you have significant assets, please use an attorney and take the time to establish an Estate Plan as well. No matter how wealthy we are, we do not want to get too isolated as we manage our finances and property. Using professionals in some roles can be advisable, but there are many common situations where having an agent act on our behalf is very beneficial for us and those we support.

Item #6: Sharing Your Health Care Information Securely

The next thing I've put in the First Folder Checklist is knowing and sharing your health care information. This is about having the legal permission to know someone's medical information. In the U.S. and Canada, there are different ways in which you give and receive this ability. HIPAA is the abbreviation used in the U.S. that stands for the Health Information Portability and Accountability Act. It simply means that you have to give people permission to know your medical information and share it with any others that need it. It's different in each health authority in Canada, so make sure that this is done in harmony with the location in which you live. And remember that, as you come into each medical facility or each medical practice, they may have their own forms that need to be filled out so that your information can be shared with the persons you desire.

> It is important for the people who will be supporting you to know all they need to know and all you want them to know as they provide and direct your care.

Sometimes this legal permission to know health information is situational. When I was taken in for surgery, a HIPAA form was filled out that gave my wife permission to get the report after the surgery and learn all the information that came from the doctor because, at that point, I would not be clear-headed enough to process that information.

But, there's also what I would call a universal permission. You can, in some places, maintain a document that gives permission to a list of people that you would want to be able to learn your health information so they can keep the people informed that you want informed. I like to maintain a HIPAA form that's used in the state of North Carolina, where I live, that has a list of my wife, my sons, their wives, and a few close friends. I keep it in my First Folder file so that, in any emergency, those with me would be able to give a copy of that to the hospital or the medical professionals taking care of me. Of course, in most of those situations, there would be forms filled out for that situation, but I don't want there to be any delay in information being passed to the people I want informed in regards to my health. Some people view it also from the other side of making sure ONLY specific people know their health care information.

To be clear. If on the day of my surgery, my wife had permission for the surgeon to give her information after my surgery, and only my son was in the room when the doctor came in to give us a report, the doctor technically would need to seek legal permission for my son to learn that information. I know health care professionals seek to share information appropriately, and everyone involved will benefit when there is clear communication and legal documents that direct the sharing of information according to your wishes.

It is important for the people who will be supporting you to know all they need to know and all you want them to know as they provide and direct your care. You do not need any permission to collect and share this information yourself. Again, it is important to know how to do this in harmony with the laws where you live.

Item #7: Emergency Contacts

The next item on the First Folder Checklist is your list of emergency contacts. I break that down into two groups. One lists your **primary emergency contacts**. Those are the people that would be contacted when you are in the midst of a crisis. They would be informed immediately that you've had a health crisis and/or need support in any way. The other includes your **secondary emergency contacts**. These are the people that need to be informed if your disability or your crisis is going to be extended.

Once the crisis has occurred and you've contacted your primary emergency contacts, the question becomes when do you move to the secondary list of emergency contacts? The basic guidance I use is a question: When do other people need to be informed? For instance, when my father continued to progress in his dementia and when he was diagnosed with cancer, it became important to inform the places that depended on him. He delivered meals to people who were homebound on Mondays for an organization called Meals on Wheels. They needed to know he wouldn't be doing his route. He also had regular volunteer hours at the USO at our airport, and they needed to know he wouldn't be there for his shift. There were other regular gatherings at three different breakfast spots. Those friends would want to know that he wouldn't be there and why. These folks were on his secondary emergency contact list.

You can imagine that, when people are depending on you or when people will be concerned about you, you would want to give them information. When my wife was going through her surgeries and cancer diagnosis, we made a group email list of those to be contacted. It wasn't a large number of people, but I didn't want to go through the process of informing everyone individually about the major points of diagnosis and prognosis. So, we used the group email and made a phone call to others.

Item #8: Location of Important Documents and Information

There are many ways to collect and share important documents and information. This item is on the checklist so you will review and share appropriately the documents in your First Folder as well as any others that you identify. There is also some information you will want to share with the appropriate people in a timely manner.

I use a cloud-based application to hold all my login and password information. There are only a few people who know how to access that information. If I am unable to direct my affairs, they will be able to do all that needs to be done until I am able to take back control or I die, when my will and Estate Plan take over.

There are many lists online and in books that will guide you through the details. Your list may be small or you may need to be thorough and focus on security if you have more assets and want to limit the risks. Do not neglect this item.

Now that we've gone through the list, I want you to see them in their short form:

1. Create a last will and testament.
2. Designate beneficiaries to your financial accounts.
3. Choose and complete the documents for your Medical POA.
4. Complete your Living Will.
5. Choose and complete the documents for your Durable POA or other POAs that are appropriate.
6. Give the appropriate people access to your medical information so they can keep the people who care about you informed as needed for their roles in your support.
7. Create your lists of Primary and Secondary Emergency Contacts.
8. Make sure the appropriate people have knowledge of and access to the items in your First Folder, as well as other important documents and information.

That's it. The First Folder Checklist has eight items that will protect you and your loved ones and provide you with more freedom than you can imagine. I recommend you use attorneys to guide you through items #1, 3, 4, and 5. There are online guides and templates if you cannot afford to work with an attorney in your local area. I don't want to list them here because they come with limitations. You can find them by doing an internet search, but it is hard to know the accuracy and risks. Having these items complete will put you among an elite group of people who have reduced their vulnerability in significant ways. I believe they are worth the time, effort and temporary anxieties.

Once you've completed the First Folder Checklist, you've only got three more things to do: 1) Secure your First Folder items. Put them in a safe place, give the appropriate people copies they may need, and let them know where they can find the originals. 2) Take note of the people who showed up in your First Folder Checklist. They are part of your Core Relationships. They will be important in the rest of this process. 3) CELEBRATE! You are part of a minority of mortals who are now less vulnerable. Seriously. Have a party! Post it for all to see! Let people know what you have done and invite them to do the same!

CHAPTER 7

Power

"Our survival depends on the healing power of love,
intimacy, and relationships. As individuals.
As a community. As a country. As a culture.
Perhaps, even as a species." — Dean Ornish, 1998

We've now arrived at the final 'P' that makes up the pieces of Life Compass Living. Thus far, we've discovered who we are as a Person, identified and engaged our People, set up base camp in our Place, and learned the Planning Process for ensuring our Person, People, and Place are Protected. Now is the time for us to understand and use our Power. Power is where the rubber meets the road when it comes to our Shared Life Vision unfolding into reality. The Dean Ornish quote above, from his book *Love & Survival,* is so powerfully true. When you dream of what's possible without the power of love, intimacy, and relationships to make it possible, it may happen, but it'll be empty. I was reminded of this while watching the movie *Bohemian Rhapsody,* the biographical drama about Freddie Mercury, the lead singer and front songwriter for the British rock band Queen. There are several scenes where Freddie is sitting in his lush Georgian mansion in London's

Kensington district, lost and alone. He had everything the material world had to offer, and yet he had nothing. As gifted and powerful as he was, he was powerless.

When you think about the power you have in your life, what do you think about? Is it money? Is it the way you look? Is it your position within a company? Is it the number of Likes, Comments, and Shares you get on a Facebook, Instagram, or Twitter post? Have you ever really thought about it?

I have to confess. I hadn't really accessed my own power. Not until the Life Quakes of my mom's cancer and my wife's cancer happened. These drove me into some dark places; places I'd never traveled as a very fortunate white middle-class male. Life sometimes has a way of shining a bright light on things we were missing while we're in the dark. It was during one of those times that I came to realize that the power I truly possess to create the life I want is grounded in my relationships, time, finances, work, and agreements. I had done well on some fronts and neglected the Power found in others.

THE POWER YOU HAVE TODAY

Once I realized the source of my Power, I created a presentation I call *The Power You Have Today*. It's an overview of how to look at your relationships, time, finances, work, and agreements as the foundational resources of your Life Compass Plan. This is one of my presentations that gets the most enthusiastic response from the widest age range. Of course, I like to be appreciated, but I especially love the conversations afterward. The most exciting parts of those conversations are the ways people describe their next steps and the questions they ask about how to take those next steps.

For example, one lady who had just turned 90 had been paying for a long-term care insurance policy for many years, and the policy had just expired. It ended on her birthday. She had spent a lot of money that she would never get back but she also never dreamed she would live to her age. She came in feeling angry, powerless and extremely vulnerable. As I talked through the process of collecting all the Power we have in the present, I saw her perk up and take notes. When I finished, she asked two specific questions. The first was about the use of life insurance to cover long-term care costs if you need the money and have a qualified life insurance policy. There are definitely ways to do this, and I was honored to point her in the right direction to learn more about doing just that. The second was about how to begin to have her Essential Conversations with her children and grandchildren. I don't remember her exact words, but she said something like, "I want them to help me if I need it, and I want to leave something to help them after I'm gone." I'm guessing her tears pointed to a hope for a Shared Life Vision and support that wasn't just about money. She was beginning to see that she had more Power to direct her own life, enrich her important relationships, and find support in the future than she had realized. She wasn't powerless just because her long-term care policy had expired. One thing I do remember her saying was, "I was about to give up. I haven't been this excited in a long time. Thank you."

At the end of another presentation a young couple in their 30s without children came up to me and said, "We definitely need to talk with our parents. We have no idea what they do and don't have in place." Their questions were about what to do if their parents weren't willing to talk with them and whether they should do their own planning before they approach their parents. I pointed them to Parallel Planning and the need to be clear on their own Life Compasses before trying to harmonize life with others. Everything is to be guided by your Life Compass!

RELATIONSHIPS: SELF, FAMILY OF CHOICE
TIME. FINANCES. WORK. AGREEMENTS.

My friend April once told me that, when she was in her 20s, the way she was able to afford her first home was through sweat equity. She made a fairly decent salary as a clinical social worker but she was far from having enough savings for a down payment on a house. She then met an investor in her church who was willing to buy the house as an investment property and hire her to help renovate it. When all was said and done with the renovation, he put the money that she earned toward the down payment and sold her the house for a profit. It took several months of hard work — painting, tearing down walls, pulling up carpet, etc. — but it was totally worth it when she signed the mortgage papers and moved in. The investor used his finances and April used her time to work. They both used their relationship and entered into an agreement with one another. It was a win-win scenario.

As you read through this chapter, I encourage you to imagine every resource (anything or anyone that meets a current or future need) that you can. Start with relationships. The whole point of Life Compass Living is to have the relationships we want with ourselves, with others, and the world. As I've said all along, the first relationship to focus on is our relationship with ourselves. Remember that the Power you have in relationship to yourself is related to how you work through your mindfulness practice, your work of deciding who you are and how you want to be in the world, and your own physical and mental vitality. Are you learning the things you want to learn so that you can understand better who you are and how you want to be in the world? How are you a resource for yourself and your role as the author of your own Life Story? My greatest challenge at the age of 62 is to learn how taking care of myself fits into my Life Compass Plan. It is embarrassing and yet, as I say it out loud, I feel the shift happening. I am learning that when I care for myself and increase my ability to accept the limitations of real life, I start flourishing much sooner and in ways that feel more like Love than those fleeting, addictive highs my "stage characters" seek from others. I am convinced that we can and do flourish as ourselves with others who need not be anything other than themselves. Is this messy and tenuous? Of course! But, oh, the adventure!

Let's keep moving! Let's move our bodies like they were made to move and expand our minds like they were made to grow! They're interrelated. So, the first resource that we're considering is ourselves, and it's the resource that we have the most control over. And if we don't have control over that resource, then that's the place to start. We must find what we need to have more of the ability to direct the resources of our own thinking, our own speaking, our own living, our own serving.

> I am convinced that we can and do flourish as ourselves with others who need not be anything other than themselves. Is this messy and tenuous? Of course! But, oh, the adventure!

The next place to look for relationship resources is in the people closest to you. Perhaps it's your life partner or spouse, or a couple of very close friends, people who are deeply committed to you and you to them. This is your Family of Choice. How do you count on these people and how do they count on you? What do you need to do to invest in these relationships? Do you need to spend more time nourishing them? If so, what do you need to give up to free up the time and space needed? Do you need to see a therapist together? Is there something blocking your connection? Something unspoken? How will you fit into one another's Life Story and Shared Life Vision and one another's legacies moving forward? In the book *Connected: The Surprising Power of Our Social Networks and How They Shape Our Lives,* Nicholas Christakis and James H. Fowler point out that our network of relationships is "a tangled pile of spaghetti weaving in and out of other paths that rarely leave the plate." What they suggest is that we have great influence on others, and others have great influence on us, but so much of the time it's unconscious. We haven't stopped to truly assess how people resource who we are and how we live or how we resource their capacity to be who they are and how they live. So begin today to look at the power you have in your current relationships.

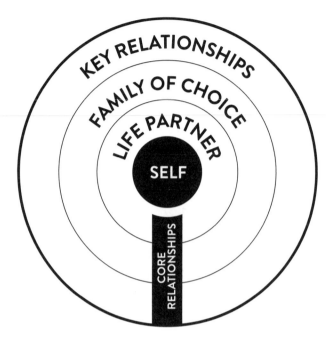

As an example, it would be obvious that I would list my wife, a handful of best friends, my faith community, and some colleagues that I work with as my people resources. When I began to work on my Life Compass Plan, I made a list of my Core Relationships. I spent several hours working on it over several days, trying to be honest and sober about it, and it still ended up being a ridiculous list. I've whittled it down to 62 people. And if you're laughing, it's appropriate. Because what we really find in studies is that the people who have a handful of relationships, perhaps just two or three, maybe as many as 15 or 20, are the ones who become secure and flourish in life. So don't think too big and too many. That's my tendency. Some people are more introverted and have a much smaller list to start with. But I'm suggesting that for all of us — introvert or extrovert — the list be very small. We need to start small so that we can consciously identify how we will resource one another's needs both today and in the future.

TIME: ESSENTIAL CONVERSATIONS
AND BEING WITH YOUR MOST IMPORTANT PEOPLE

The second place to think about Power is time. Some people say that time isn't real. And I guess that is true, philosophically. It might not be a concrete reality. But the truth is, time is the space where relationships happen. Time is never empty. Time can be spent poorly, but it is always moving, and we are spending that finite resource in ways that do or do not help our ability to flourish and to have what we need.

So one question to ask in terms of the Power of time is, how do we share time? To know the Power of Life Compass Living you will need to make time for your Essential Conversations. When you feel insecure, lonely, or depressed you may find great help in your Essential Conversations. If you are feeling strong, ready to flourish, and content, I'll bet it is because you know who you are and how you fit in your Life Story. Even if you call them something else, you know your Life Compass and have others you can count on. Time spent in Essential Conversations is like coming to agree on the compass that guides your adventure. Until that happens, how will you go together?

One of the places you share a lot of time is in housing. As you begin to imagine Power in terms of time, who are the people you live with? In the scenario of my friend Jamie, who moved into a multi-generational home with his partner and parents, the time he's saved by not having to drive to his parents' home, pick them up, take them to appointments, drive them home, and then drive himself home is significant. Plus, there's no driving time when they have family get-togethers. The move not only increased their financial resources,

> Time spent in Essential Conversations is like coming to agree on the compass that guides your adventure. Until that happens, how will you go together?

it increased the time resources they have with one another and with others in their Outer Circles of Connection. Jamie can now spend more time with Anne and with their friends. He can spend more time meditating and exercising. He can spend more time writing music.

Who are the people you want to spend more time with? Are there adjustments you need to make to reduce the distance between you so that you can spend more time together? And if that's not possible, is there something you can do to generate more financial and time resources to allow you to see one another more often? What about using technology to facilitate spending more time together? There's an article in the November 2019 issue of The Atlantic that I found fascinating. The title of it is *Why You Never See Your Friends Anymore: Our unpredictable and overburdened schedules are taking a dire toll on American society.* The author, Judith Shulevitz, points out the reality that many of us are living with unpredictable work schedules. And we have so many social connections, we are not able to connect deeply with the people that we want and need in our lives in order to be secure. Per Shulevitz, "A calendar is more than the organization of days and months. It's the blueprint for how a shared life happens." Truth!

Time is a finite resource. How much any of us has left is unknown. Are you spending your time wisely? Are you carving out time for yourself and those you love? Where are your time priorities? What adjustments do you need to make, if any? How will you and your people spend your time resources? The reason I point to time after relationships is you have to set aside that resource in order to be with the people the way you want to be with them. So, look at the resource of time and use it with one another.

FINANCES: BUDGET, SAVINGS, AND SHARING.

The next resource is finances. In looking at our needs today and/or planning our future, this is the place most Americans want to start. We tend to think maybe, if we make ourselves comfortable and secure as consumers, we'll be comfortable and secure today. But as has been told by many philosophers, spiritual teachers, and my grandpa on many occasions, money can't make you happy, but it can sure help you enjoy the happy life you've got.

How do we share our finances? It's a real question. Some of us will decide to share our finances and some of us won't. Money is a funny thing. Some people don't want to talk about it. They don't want to openly share how much they have or how much they owe. I was taught to not ask people how much something cost. I have broken that rule and learned why it exists. It usually causes me to make a judgment based on far too little knowledge and as I was told, "It's none of your business." It is not my business until it is. We need to let others guide how we know them and how we share life with them. Don't neglect finances and don't let them come before or between your relationships! Let your Essential Conversations help you discover the best way to use your money to resource your Life Compass Plan.

So when it comes to the resource of finances within our Life Compass Plan and Shared Life Vision, first take time to Discover one another and, during the Determine and Define stages, you can learn how people feel about talking about money. Simply ask the question, "Are we going to share finances and, if so, how?" Support, as you remember, flows in both directions. There are people we'll support financially and those who either have supported or will support us. If you have people who don't want to talk about money, you'll have to do the best you can to Parallel Plan for if and when they need financial assistance. Perhaps finances will never be an issue for them as far as paying for services during the Mutual Care and Dependent Care phases of their life. (Remember these can start at any age.) Keep in mind, though, that, even with full-time formal caregivers, you may need to manage or provide care to some degree. Family caregivers contribute huge amounts of money to our economy by not being paid. The value of services provided, in the United States alone, by informal caregivers has steadily increased over the past decade, with an estimated economic value of $470 billion in 2013, up from $450 billion in 2009 and $375 billion in 2007. At $470 billion, the value of unpaid caregiving exceeded the value of paid home care and total Medicaid spending in 2013, and nearly matched the value of the sales of the world's largest company, Walmart ($477 billion). [AARP Public Policy Institute. (2015). Valuing the Invaluable: 2015 Update.]

So remember, in terms of finances, that often people are contributing a huge amount of value that protects finances when they become caregivers in the many ways people provide care. One of the greatest emotional struggles family caregivers face is resentment. How are you going to feel spending your time on someone in your Family of Choice when they haven't been willing to spend their finances on you, or vice versa? These are hard discussions that you'll need to have during your Essential Conversations. Do the best you can to do these two things: Get clear on the finances that actually exist for today and tomorrow, and put the legal paperwork in place to protect it.

WORK

I want to encourage us all to acknowledge each person's work as we have our Essential Conversations and form Life Compass Plans. Notice both vocations and avocations. Seek to fully value the work that comes with an income and the work that holds value by meeting needs and making it possible for you all to flourish without the transfer of currency. Many people do their jobs, go to work, in order to help themselves and their Family of Choice have what they need. Some of my heroes grind out their days hoping for jobs that are a better fit for their Life Compass but shoulder on because their Life Compass Plan needs them to. I have spoken to this above, but the Power you share often comes from work that is undervalued and unappreciated. When you define your roles and delegate responsibilities in your Essential Conversations, take the time to value and appreciate each person's work.

As I began adulting in the 1970s, there was a big shift happening in the role of women. I remember our culture struggling with how to value and supply what had been the "unpaid" work done in the home, communities, and extended family, primarily by women. In 1978, it included the household taking shape as Tammy and I began negotiating the roles within our nuclear family. I remember a day after we got back to campus housing (we were juniors in college) from our honeymoon and started doing our five part-time jobs around classes and studies. We came home from classes and settled down in our 600-square-foot trailer, and I asked, "What's for dinner?". I woke up to the awareness that Tammy did not have the same division of labor in mind that my mother had. She replied, "Whatever you want to fix." Needless to say, even though we didn't call it that, our Essential Conversations began in earnest, and we learned to have clarity on a Shared Life Vision and value all the ways we each contributed to our Life Compass Plan. The wisdom we learned was, "Try not to get trapped in the roles that no longer support your Shared Life Vision." As we have taken our annual anniversary getaway I mentioned earlier, we have modified our Shared Life Vision at least 42 times. WORK. WORK. WORK. It is a great adventure that remains messy and tenuous and demands work.

Notice work in all its forms as you learn to flourish together in every stage of life and manage life transitions with elegance. I am encouraged to see so many voices entering our awareness that show us the value of having passions, serving others, and informing our lives. I see social media inviting us to follow people who are showing us how to find, develop, and share our "work." Tammy and I follow people who help us save a lot of time getting

Try not to get trapped in the roles that no longer support your Shared Life Vision.

better at the work we are paid for and the work that pays off in our Life Compass Plan.

AGREEMENTS: FAMILY OF CHOICE

The final resource is the agreements we have with one another. In most of human history, there were numerous agreements shared without a need to negotiate them. These were shared with our families, clans, tribes, faith communities, neighbors, and other memberships we maintained in various groups and organizations. It may take some imagination, but I encourage us to open our minds to the ways humans have made one another secure by having agreements implicit and explicit in these networks of mutuality.

Family, in its many expressions, has included some guarantees along with the dysfunctions. I have seen spouses, parents, and relatives help one another through real-life challenges without needing to ask "if" they would show up, and help even if there was some degree of angst as they decided "how" to show up. Life Compass Living helps us decide who our Family of Choice will be, so those promises can be made and kept even as we affirm individual freedoms and make room for the many ways families take shape in the world as it is.

An article in the March 2020 edition of The Atlantic made a bold statement that may not be true for everyone reading this book, but it is obviously true for some of us. It was titled *The Nuclear Family was a Mistake*. The author, David Brooks, says, "The shift from bigger and interconnected extended families to smaller and detached nuclear families ultimately led to a familial system that liberates the rich and ravages the working-class and the poor." The causes were "economic, cultural, and institutional all at once." He claims that extended families, hear larger Family of Choice, have two great strengths: resilience and socialization. My parents, grandparents and relatives talked of how they got through the tough times together. I also remember being parented, directed, and disciplined by many adults in my extended family, as well as some neighbors who seemed to be doing just what my folks would have done if they had witnessed the occasion that necessitated some type of intervention. Brooks observes that the ones who have lost the most with the shift to the nuclear family have been children and older adults. However, people of all ages are looking for a shift in the way we do family in order to address the confusion and ambivalence. He encourages us to form what he calls "forged families." I agree. I am happy for those who still have or can reclaim an extended family that is multi-generational and has the proximity to show up for one another. I would title my article *The Nuclear Family Can't Do It All!* Tammy and I cannot flourish without our Family of Choice. I hope we all stop trying as we are set free from the lie of the independent self and the romanticized fantasy of a nuclear family being sufficient.

When you are looking for the resources held in your Family of Choice, I encourage you to use your Essential Conversations to make explicit any agreements that you may assume are present and implicit. You will gain a growing awareness of who is going to share life with you, along with how they will share life and what they will bring to the adventure. This may include disappointments but, over time, you will forge a security found in a family ready to celebrate the good times and navigate the storms. A friend of mine, who was caring for her aunt, told her she'd "always have her back." And she did. So much so that, when her aunt died in the hospital, my friend turned the air down in her hospital room and sat with her body until the funeral home staff arrived. It took them close to six hours to get there. Once they arrived and put her aunt on the gurney, my friend followed them to the hearse. She made sure she had her aunt's back until the last minute. This was an agreement she made and kept. There are also babies that will be arriving who want to know their People and Place will not only celebrate their arrival but help them grow up in a Family of Choice where they flourish in every stage of life and navigate life transitions with elegance.

There may only be a few who share a lot of details about their Life Compass and all the resources they bring to be shared. Let the process unfold as you all move along the Trajectory of Readiness and prepare in and outside the urgency of Life Transitions and Life Quakes.

AGREEMENTS: THE OUTER CIRCLES OF CONNECTION

Another collection of agreements we share (if we are fortunate enough for it to be true) are found in the communities, states, provinces, and nations where we live and are citizens. We call those our Outer Circles of Connection. We shape the benefits of community and citizenship with our voices and votes, as well as our own ways of being neighbors. Many people stay and relocate to participate in the resources held in these agreements. They are collected and distributed in many ways. Some involve taxes, dues, donations, volunteering, and more. The list is far too large to be included here.

Some important resources to be aware of are what I call programs, products, and services. As you have your Essential Conversations and begin gathering your resources, be aware of the programs, products, and services that are available where you live and from the groups you participate in. Some you currently use, and others you'll need in the future. Tell the folks in your Essential Conversations and Family of Choice which ones you're using and find out which ones they're using, if any.

Knowing this is important for several reasons. The first is in case there's an emergency. You'll want to ensure that the folks who will support you can get in touch with whomever it is delivering the service, to inform them of the emergency. For example, the names and numbers for physicians, pastors/priests/rabbis, school administration, etc.

The second reason is because the program, product, or service may benefit someone else in your Family of Choice. This is more of a lighthearted example, but I've watched one group of folks share the same hairdresser, lawn person, financial planner, and funeral home director. Once one of them discovers a program, product, or service that's affordable and high quality, they all share in the discovered treasure.

The third reason is because some programs, products, and services have stipulations that can be inadvertently impacted in a negative way by well-meaning people wanting to share a Life Compass Plan. For example, I know a family who became aware of a need for a disabled member of their family who had become an adult. He was in a program that served his disability. He was in a group home, and the group home costs were covered by a program that was supported by the government. It was a public program, and it was based on disability and financial need. A family member heard about the need and wrote that disabled adult a big check. The additional money jeopardized how he qualified for the program, and he could have had to move out of the group home in which he was settled and happy. It was because there wasn't an awareness of what services were being provided or how the qualification happened. So, even when people want to do things to support one another, it's good for us to understand how the resource and the Power we have with it actually works.

Another reason to take stock in programs, products, and services as you begin your Essential Conversations is that there are often resources that are missed, as well as some unique to your location. After working with people in several states in the United States and two provinces of Canada, I've learned that the resources are very different — and even the vocabulary describing those resources is different. So, it's very important when you're collecting the Power you have and the resources you have access to, to become aware of what's available to you all and how those resources can be accessed.

Next, as you begin to discover the Power you have in time, finances, and agreements within your relationships, you'll be better able to ensure you're getting the maximum benefit out of the programs, products, and services that are out there. When I knew that my dad qualified for some in-home health care and I understood exactly how many hours he qualified for and what services would be provided, I could then plan around that. It was in understanding what the service was, how it would be provided, and when that I began to use their services better and I could let the people in my Core Relationships know when I needed their help. This reduced my load and gave the gift of helping to others who became caregivers for my dad.

Lastly, finding and understanding the plethora of programs, products, and services available takes research. It often takes specialized knowledge, and we need to spend the time early on understanding what is available not only within the relationships we have, but in the place where we live, our community.

As I've gone through this process, I've created forms that are available on the Life Compass Living website that you can download, print, and use to collect and share this information. There are also secure cloud-based platform services like Everplans.com joincake.com, and legacyarmour.com that are available, where you can collect and share information with one another via the internet. I encourage you to take the time to do this exercise. Make it a fun thing. Have folks over. Then get your phones out and create an online account or download the forms from the Life Compass Living website and fill them in. If you choose to go the paper route, invest in a large hardback notebook and have everyone doodle something fun on it ... or take a group picture and tape it to the cover. Be creative. Maybe even name your tribe. This is an adventure you're mapping out. Enjoy the planning process. Take note of the collective power and energy you feel as each person settles into a shared reality so that you truly "have each other's backs"

Reading this book means you are part of the Life Compass Living Community! Remember our shared mission:

We help one another flourish in every stage of life, and manage life transitions with elegance. We do that by helping one another have our Essential Conversations and create a Life Compass Plan to build the lives we want, with the People we want, in the Place we want. We help one another put that Plan together and find the resources to make it a reality.

Since you have made a purchase from us … you are an INSIDER now!

Here are some ways we will support you and help you find others in the Life Compass Living Community to encourage, inform, and share the progress we make. I'm still working on my own Life Compass Plan every day!

FREE RESOURCES

- INSIDER Website resources — We have worksheets, forms, and other resources on our website. All you have to do to access them is to fill out a short reader survey and share your email address so we can stay in touch. (You can unsubscribe if you wish, but we believe you'll find a lot that will help you and the People you love.)

- INSIDER FaceBook Page — We will share live events, mutual encouragement, and limited access to the Life Compass Living Team.
- INSIDER Tools for Life Compass Living — You will receive emails with curated content and the latest news before others get it.
- INSIDER Digital Gatherings — We will use Zoom and other platforms to get together, learn, and celebrate our progress in Life Compass Living!
- You will also receive INSIDER bonuses and discounts!

Thank you for sharing the journey of Life Compass Living with us! We hope to see you soon!

APPENDIX ONE

The GOAL/NEED Form

GOAL-NEED:

PRIORITY
☐ Urgent
☐ Crucial
☐ Beneficial
☐ Desireable
☐ Worth considering

READINESS
☐ Moving on it
☐ Preparing to move
☐ Getting informed
☐ Considering it
☐ On the shelf

COMPLETION DEADLINE:

NEXT STEP:

NEXT STEP DEADLINE:

INFORMATION NEEDED:

PEOPLE INVOLVED/RESPONSIBLE:

_____   _____

_____   _____

_____   _____

CONVERSATIONS/DECISIONS NEEDED:

PROFESSIONALS NEEDED:

_____   _____

_____   _____

_____   _____

I want to walk through using the Goal/Need form in order to offer a process of moving forward that honors everyone and keeps those who are having their Essential Conversations and building a Life Compass Plan together and focused. If you have a process of life or time management that works for you, use it. Remember to also have a process that others can share with you. I do not offer this as a perfect or best process. But I hope you will read this and utilize all that is useful for your Essential Conversations and Life Compass Planning.

Remember the progressions that inform the lists below:

1. Inside/Out — Start at the center of your Circles of Connection, thus Self to Life Partner to Household to Family of Choice to Core Relationships. The direction of your Life Compass Plan comes from the center and the needs of those people and relationships come first.

2. Basic Needs to Flourishing — Make sure the basic needs of your most important people and relationships are met before or as you direct resources to the hopes you share that enable you to flourish together.

3. Current to Future Needs — It is obvious that you would start with current needs, but go ahead and collect the future needs you hope to meet with resources you make available over time. Consider future needs along with current needs so that you do not dedicate more resources than those needed to the current needs so you can dedicate and grow the resources available to your Family of Choice in the future.

I want you to use this form to keep your three lists.

1. Priority Actions — This is a short list of the tasks you are doing next. This can include any part of follow-through and, as you accomplish them, look to bring items from the others lists to move on to next.

2. Progressive Plans — This is the collection of all you decide is worthy of working on in the future. You will use the form to prioritize the list as you progress in your Essential Conversations and Life Compass Planning. The top of the list will be those tasks you have decided are urgent or crucial and actionable. You will move them to your Priority Action list when you choose.

3. Periodic Review — You will decide when to review each item in order to stay current with yourself and others in your Essential Conversations. The items at the top of the list will need to be reviewed more frequently. I suggest reviewing your entire list, as well as your First Folder Checklist, once a year.

I will describe what goes in each part of the form and then give five examples. The same five examples will be used throughout the form.

GOAL/NEED

This is the place to simply **name what you are hoping to accomplish**. This is what motivates your progress on the Trajectory of Readiness. You will decide how important and how urgent each item is, but please collect everything you discover that is worth working toward. You may want to collect all your goals and needs and then move the ones you choose to the form or your own process of follow-through. You can identify them as you work on your own Life Story and Life Compass.

Examples:
- Write a short version of your Life Story to share.
- Find the resources to have a budget with savings for your household.
- Build a Shared Life Vision with your life partner.
- Stabilize Mom's life after her stroke.
- Solidify a plan for each child to have a profession that can supply their needs and utilize their gifts.

PRIORITY

This is where you honestly decide if something is:

Worth considering — and thus should be kept on a list to review.

- Desirable — and could then be included in your Essential Conversations but may not take up much time and resources for now.
- Beneficial — and is worthy of the actions to formally take through your Essential Conversations so you can know if and when to include them in your Life Compass Plan.
- Crucial — and is needed as part of your Essential Conversations and Life Compass Plan.
- Urgent — and will claim the focused attention of your Essential Conversations and Life Compass Planning. Notice who agrees on the urgency and has the ability to move things forward.

Examples:

- Having a Life Story is crucial since your Family of Choice needs to include the real you and is beginning Essential Conversations together.
- A budget with savings is urgent because it needs to be a goal that always has a next step that is being worked on.
- Having a Shared Life Vision with your most important relationship is crucial since it needs to guide your Essential Conversations and Life Compass Plan. It is likely that you have a functioning version that brought you together and keeps you together. It will be urgent if the relationship is in crisis.
- Stabilizing Mom's life is urgent if you are responsible for her care and need her crisis to be addressed in order to stay true to your Life Compass.

- A plan for a child's profession is desirable when he/she is young and you are still discovering who he/she is becoming. Homework is urgent as part of this goal. Essential Conversations will be crucial and need to start early as you invite her/him to own their own becoming, author their Life Story and define their Life Compass. A desirable Goal or future Need is there to review and update in your Essential Conversations.

READINESS

This is a progression from the bottom of the list, On the shelf, to the top of the list, Moving on it. It will prove very helpful to be aware of the honest assessment of readiness for yourself and each person in your Essential Conversations and Life Compass Plan. You will see the need to use Parallel Planning when you are compelled to move and others are not. Moving through this progression together is the hope but need not impede the progress that is urgent and possible.

Examples:

- You may be preparing to move on writing your Life Story by mindfully deciding the wisdom or spiritual practice that will guide you. Thought Partners will be important. When you are ready, or when you want to see if you are ready, then you will start moving on to actually writing your Life Story to share.
- You may be getting informed as you find a person or a process that teaches you how to make and follow a budget. You will be preparing to move as you learn how and then begin moving on it as you build the budget. You may need to seek a better job, reduce your spending, or share resources with others as part of getting to this goal. I have done them all.

- You may be preparing to move on building a Shared Life Vision by learning the Essential Conversations process and getting some clarity on your own Life Compass. You may find that you are already moving on it in your relationship and will simply let Life Compass Living expand and focus your ongoing love and vision.

- Stabilizing Mom's life will have tasks that need to be done, so you will always be moving on something but you will want to pay attention to how each part of meeting her needs can benefit from getting informed and preparing to move. Caregivers often burn out because they stay in the urgent and moving on it dance that fails to utilize all the Power available.

- Parents will need to spend years getting informed for the overall goal of helping their children find their Place in the world. Parenting in Life Compass Living will encourage Essential Conversations that invite and teach young people to practice telling their Life Story and see the Life Compass Plan they are part of. This will help them appreciate the many ways in which their People celebrate and cultivate them as a Person and provide the resources for the Place so they can flourish.

COMPLETION DEADLINE

This is a date that is set together when possible and by yourself when needed. Having a date indicates you have chosen to take it off the shelf and start making progress. If it involves others and/or causes a significant amount of anxiety to get the desired outcome, let the date move out as part of your Essential Conversations. If you choose to leave it blank, go back, and reconsider the priority and readiness that may explain why choosing a date needs to wait.

Examples:

- The completion date for having your Life Story ready to share could be months ahead. Having a date is something to tell those you hope to share it with. This will let them know your intention to more fully participate in your Essential Conversations and invite them to have the same goal with a completion date.

- When you have decided on the budgeting process you will use, you may want to have a completion date of three months so you can have a full understanding of your expenses, spending habits, and potential for additional income or saving through sharing resources.

- A completion date for your Shared Life Vision with your life partner could be your next anniversary and you could then protect time to work on it. If you get to the anniversary with work left to do you can recommit to the work and enjoy the progress your have made. It is a continuing process in my experience.

- You may see that you and your Family of Choice will need two months to learn all the resources available and work through your Essential Conversations that address Mom's needs. The urgency may leave less time for Life Compass Planning than you would want, but if you can share a deadline with those who wish to support Mom, it will help you become more efficient with the time you have.

- It may seem obvious that the deadline for a child to choose a profession is age 18, but remember what I shared about Adulting in our world. I would suggest that the first deadline could be age 12 and that the young person helps you decide the next deadline they could work toward. If they

have their own Life Compass Plan early, they can participate in choosing how to utilize the limited resources for
their People. As my children started seeing professions to
pursue I introduced them to people who were doing it so
they could see the preparations needed, the lifestyle is supported, and the actual cost of living as that kind of professional. (I changed my major a few times in college because
I was doing these experiments on my own. And remember that following our Life Compass Plan will prepare us
for Life Compass Plan 2.0, 3.0, or maybe even 10.0. I've
had 12 rebirths in my life that reframed my world view. I
am grateful for each one and I hope to get to the next one
ASAP. Life Compass Living is an adventure, not a march.)

NEXT STEP

Make this specific and share it with everyone who will participate in
accomplishing the step. You will know when a step needs to be broken
down into smaller steps, but hold onto what needs to happen to move up
the progression of readiness and toward the outcomes you have determined
will help you flourish together.

Examples:
- The next step in preparing to share your Life Story could
  be to set aside a day in a space that is peaceful so you can
  write or dictate your Life Story to yourself and your Higher
  Power or Compassionate Listener. You can look for what is
  in the story you tell later. As much as possible, give yourself the freedom to tell YOUR STORY. It is the first job of
  Life Compass Living. You may want to do this with your
  life partner or a Thought Partner, if that will help you get

it out. Look for ways you can grow into owning your story and choosing what is for others to know based on where they are in your Circles of Connection.

- The next step in budgeting could be to buy a notebook and get out a pen to start recording everything you spend money on and who could help you increase your income or share resources with you.
- The next action for building a Shared Life Vision with my life partner could be to schedule a day — or two, or three — to go away and see where you are in your Essential Conversations. You may realize you have a lot of clarity on some things and you will benefit greatly from knowing you have the clarity you want.
- The next step toward stabilizing Mom's life after her stroke could be to move into her home with her, so you can make sure she has what she needs, fully assess the current and future needs, and involve her as much as possible in the Essential Conversations and Life Compass Planning her Family of Choice is doing for her.
- The next step to solidify a plan for each child to have a profession that can supply their needs and utilize their gifts will be determined by many factors. But it could be to read a book with your child that tells a story that spurs on the Essential Conversations he or she is ready to have. My experience is that the classic children's books are made for that. I will include the favorites of my People in the bibliography.

NEXT STEP DEADLINE

Choose a deadline that you are committed to and keep everyone informed who is helping meet the deadline.

INFORMATION NEEDED

Make a list of what you need to learn in order to move up the progression of readiness. Include the location of that information, if you know it.

Examples:

- To write a short version of your Life Story to share, you could make a list of the important questions for you to answer so you can own your role as the Author. These could include "Who or what guides the Plot of my Life Story?" "Who do I want to keep in my Life Story?" "Where do I hope my Life Story takes me in the next five years?" "What is in my Backstory that I need to include or exclude from the Storyline moving forward?"
- There will be a lot of information needed to find the resources to have a budget with savings for your household. Stay focused on what gets you to a balanced budget sooner and let the amount of savings grow as you have your Essential Conversations and form your Life Compass Plan.
- As you build a Shared Life Vision with your life partner, Essential Conversations will serve as a source for the information you need.
- There will be a significant amount of information needed to find and access the resources to stabilize Mom's life after her stroke. You will be learning who can help and how they can help. You will also be looking for the resources in the Agreements I talked about. When a person needs help because of limited finances, insufficient family support, physical disability, or limited cognitive function, there are a host of options that will only be discovered with research, assertiveness, or the help of professionals. Make it a team research project as much as possible.

- Let your mind open up to all the information you need to solidify a plan for each child to have a profession that can supply their needs and utilize their gifts. I believe there are many ways that parents can utilize the skills of LERA from Chapter 3 as they have their ongoing Essential Conversations with their blossoming in-house storyteller.

PEOPLE INVOLVED/RESPONSIBLE

This is an invitational process of including all who will help direct and accomplish, or be impacted, as you reach the goals or meet the needs you are working toward. It is also where you identify who is willing and able to be responsible for the tasks that must be done.

Examples:
- Find the people you need to help you write a short version of your Life Story to share. You are the one responsible for this goal. Let them inform, encourage, and explore the story you tell.
- Sorting out who to involve and who is responsible as you find the resources to have a budget with savings for your household will be important. Remember Facts, Power, and Ability. Focus on those who have the power to secure or share resources. The most responsible will be those in your household and any who agree to be part of your Life Compass Plan.
- Building a Shared Life Vision with my life partner is a shared responsibility. You will involve your People as you choose, but it is yours to build.
- Sorting out who to involve and who is responsible as you stabilize Mom's life after her stroke could be complex, but do not neglect to make this list. Mom may not be able to

accept the responsibilities for her own care, and it may take time and effort to establish who will be part of her care team and what responsibilities each person will accept. Be as faithful to the Essential Conversations process as possible, but ask all those who are appropriate to become involved and responsible for some part of Mom's Life Compass Plan.

- As you solidify a plan for each child to have a profession that can supply their needs and utilize their gifts, you will involve many people, but primarily those who have the power to define and direct the young person. Teachers, coaches, mentors, and friends will join and leave the team as you and your children direct all the actions and resources that supply and shape this goal. Over time, the responsibility will belong to each child who learns to do their own Adulting and follow their own Life Compass Plan.

CONVERSATIONS/DECISIONS NEEDED

Since Life Compass Living is focused on relationships and personal responsibility, this is where you work to let your progress be directed and unfold in and through Essential Conversations and Life Compass Planning. This is not perfect, but it helps everyone remain involved as their lives and resources support the lives of others. Let the conversations and decisions impact the deadlines even as they seek to meet the deadlines.

Examples:

- As you prepare to write a short version of my Life Story to share, you will need to have the conversations with yourself (mindfulness) and make the decisions that are yours. Each of the conversations and decisions may need to involve others, but work to become more fully present and participatory in choosing and working through them.
- You may need to have conversations with those in your household to find the resources they bring — or may be able to bring — to building a budget with savings for the household they share with you. You may have to do some hard work deciding to limit expenses or share property, space, and time.
- Essential Conversations will help you build a Shared Life Vision with your life partner. They will include appropriate decisions.
- You may need to be assertive with those who are willing to support the goal to stabilize Mom's life after her stroke. It is fair, especially when needs are urgent, to insist on conversations and decisions. Remember to continue Parallel Planning in order to hold onto your own self-determination. Making sure everyone on the care team knows the conversations and decisions that are needed will help uti-

lize any mutual regard shared by those who want Mom to have her needs met and have their own Life Compasses honored in the process.

- The work to solidify a plan for each child to have a profession that can supply their needs and utilize their gifts is an ongoing process of conversations and decisions. Make this list in light of where each Person is in their own development and ability to accept personal responsibility. The Trajectory of Readiness can help you all remain patient and ready to increase your shared awareness and acceptance.

PROFESSIONALS NEEDED

This is where you collect the professionals that will help you have your Essential Conversations, make your Life Compass Plan, and find the resources to make your Life Compass Plan a reality. The hope is to use professionals only when they can help you save time, save money, expand your ability to enrich your relationships or secure your life by avoiding Life Quakes and supplying the needs of your Life Transitions. Make sure the professionals honor your Life Compass Plan and are worth the time and money they cost.

Examples:

- You may want the help of a counselor, spiritual director, life coach, or teacher to write a short version of your Life Story to share. I used them all to fill in my Life Story, even as I owned the story as it developed.
- In order to find the resources to have a budget with savings for your household, you may want to pay a small amount for access to a budgeting system with teachers and a community that will help you implement it well. I have recently found help from the app and online resources

of You Need a Budget. I benefited greatly from Financial Peace University by Dave Ramsey and the Clark Howard radio show in the past. The hope is that you will become ready to use many other professionals as you dedicate resources to your future needs and ability to flourish.

- It is good to know how to utilize the professionals who have proven their ability to help people build what we call a Shared Life Vision with a life partner. Tammy and I have used a marriage and family therapist. We have thoroughly enjoyed and benefited from participating in marriage enrichment events. It was money and time well-spent. We could not afford to buy one-on-one time with those professionals, but we could learn from their teaching, group work, and writing. Brene Brown has been helping us a lot lately, and we have never met her.

- It may not be possible to stabilize Mom's life after her stroke with the help of professionals. Remember we are in a caregiver shortage. Utilizing professional caregivers and the host of other professionals who direct the programs, products, and services you discover in this process can be a very time-consuming role. Let others help you make this list and then work to keep it current with those you need and can afford.

- You may think that, as you solidify a plan for each child to have a profession that can supply their needs and utilize their gifts, you do not need professionals. This is not so. These may include teachers in school, music teachers, and a host of other professional teachers who help your children discover and develop their minds, talents, and skills. This could also include some professional assessments that help you know the gifts and challenges of each child. When we learned about the dyslexia of our son and how to turn that challenge into an asset, he was able to excel in the areas of his passions. He is doing post-doctorate work in his passion that would have been much less likely without the gift of all that professional taught us.

Do not turn this form into a burden. My hope is that it will help you decide what to include in your Essential Conversations and Life Compass Planning and then help you with your follow-through. Remember to bring your own honesty, responsibility, and compassion as you use LERA and you will learn to flourish together.

The StoryBrand Vision

This is how we view our hopes for the Life Compass Living Community. It is a model developed using insights from Donald Miller and the StoryBrand Model of Marketing. This is a sincere effort to be honest about the commitments we make as the Life Compass Living Team. We are people who need and seek what we offer. We can only do it together.

1. **A Character: They want to know how to flourish, live the life they want, with the people they want in the place they want. A plan for today and a secure future.**

2. **Has a Problem:**

   a. Villain: The current or future crisis (job loss, Mom's fall, economic shift, relationship trouble, or pandemic) that invades life and decimates our future.

      i. External: We need to have the people and resources to live the life we really want.

      ii. Internal: We hate those moments when we feel scared, inadequate, confused, or toxic for those we care about. We want to live well, flourish, and cause flourishing.

iii. Philosophical: We want to have a life and legacy we choose that includes those we love and helps us progress toward our shared hopes.

3. And meets a Guide:

Empathy: We (the LCL team) have faced off with the challenges that come as we seek to flourish and help others flourish. We want to share what we have learned and learn from your (the clients') progress. We want allies in the adventure of learning to flourish today and secure our futures together.

Authority: We have done the research (since 2013), learned from life, and worked with more than 300 people, as well as businesses and faith communities, who have used our tools, improved on those tools, and realized more of the life they really wanted. We seek allies and not just customers.

4. Who gives them a Plan:

Process: The Life Compass Plan — This shows you how to have Essential Conversations and translate the hopes you discover into the life you want with the people you want to go where you want.

Agreement: We will only work for you (no hidden referral fees and exclusive partnerships), give you the vision to consider and share (you can do a lot before you purchase our services), asking you to pay only for what you can use today, and invite you to help improve how the Life Compass Living Community can flourish together.

5. And calls them to Action:

Direct: Get started NOW! We are ready to help you with a growing list of educational resources and your own Life Compass Facilitator.

Transitional: Learn more! We will let you know through email more about the why and the what of Life Compass Living even before we offer the services that support you planning how and finance our work for you.

6. **That ends in Success:** You will have more of the life you really want, deeper connections with the people you love, and build a legacy that is a gift to those you want to help flourish.

7. **Helps them Avoid a failure:** You will refuse to waste your time, your resources, and your relationships chasing things you do not value only to end up lonely and afraid as your journey ends.

8. **Character Transformation:**

From: Frustrated with my current insecurities, where my life is going and scared about how I will deal with the coming crises that are part of real-life and cost a lot of money, time, and emotional energy.

To: I am moving into the life I want, with the people I want, toward the future we want with a plan for how we will manage the transitions and the potential crises that are part of normal life and within the elegant use of our shared resources.

APPENDIX THREE

A Quick Reference Tool Box for Life Compass Living

LIFE COMPASS LIVING

LIFE COMPASS

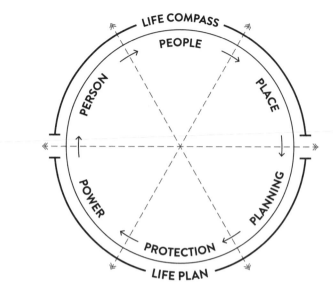

LIFE COMPASS

PEOPLE

PERSON

PLACE

POWER

PLANNING

PROTECTION

LIFE PLAN

**CHAPTER 2:
LIFE STORY MODEL**

Plot

CIRCLES OF
CONNECTION

Backstory

Author

Storyline
(in media res)

Characters

CORE RELATIONSHIPS

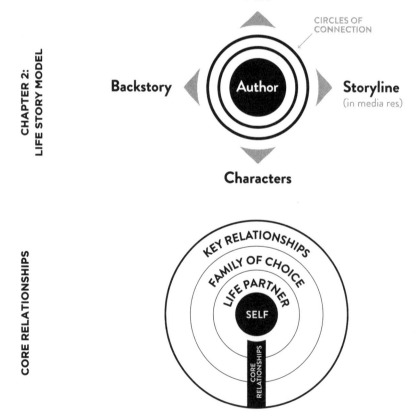

KEY RELATIONSHIPS

FAMILY OF CHOICE

LIFE PARTNER

SELF

CORE
RELATIONSHIPS

First Half of Life

Forming Ages 18-26	Growing Ages 26-35	Launching Ages 36-45	Influencing Ages 45-60
Discovery Excitement Validation	Success	Balance & Health	Meaning Spirituality Community

Second Half of Life (Eldering)

Transitioning Ages 61-80	Mutual Care (IADLs)	Dependent Care (ADLs)
Influencing Commitment Connected	Savoring Legacy Companionship	Presence

FACTS ◈ POWER ◈ ABILITY
◈ SHARED LIFE VISION ◈
◈ PARALLEL PLANNING ◈

Glossary

Adulting — An informal term to describe behavior that is seen as responsible and grown-up. This behavior often involves meeting the mundane demands of independent and professional living, such as paying bills and running errands.

Adventure — Participation in exciting undertakings or enterprises, usually a risky undertaking; of uncertain outcome. I use it as a proactive approach to the messy and tenuous nature of life.

Author — In the Life Story Model, the author is the person whose Life Story is unfolding. The hope is that each of us will own the role of shaping the story that is ours.

Care Team — A support group sharing the journey with people fighting to live well while battling sickness, disability, or death.

Circles of Connection — A Circle of Connection provides a framework for managing expectations, roles, and resources on an emotional and practical level. It also helps define who you are in relation to others and your world.

Core Relationships — Within the Circles of Connection, our Core Relationships include ourselves, our life partner, our Family of Choice, and other Key Relationships. These are the relationships to focus on in a Life Compass Plan so that all other relationships maintain fidelity to them.

Dignity of Choice — This is a basic value in Life Compass Living, which insists that the autonomy and wishes of every person be honored and expressed in our Essential Conversations and Life Compass Planning.

Elder — I use the term elder to mean those people who hold the stories and places of honor in their communities and are valued as sources of wisdom.

Essential Conversations — Talking to the most important people about the most important things in our lives. As part of Life Compass Planning introduced in this book, they include four stages. Discover, Determine, Define, and Delegate.

FOMO (Fear Of Missing Out) — The anxiety that an exciting or interesting event may currently be happening elsewhere, often aroused by posts seen on a social media website.

Formal caregivers — aid care providers providing care in one's home or in a care setting (daycare, residential facility, long-term care facility).

Framily — The good friends who are not related to us and become part of the family we choose for ourselves.

Generativity — A concern for the future, a need to nurture and guide younger people and contribute to the next generation. Psychologist Erik Erikson argued that this usually develops during middle age (which spans ages 40 through 64) in keeping with his stage-model of psychosocial development.

Home — Where our Life Story and contributions are valued, supported, and expressed.

Hospice care — A type of health care that focuses on the palliation of a terminally ill patient's pain and symptoms and attending to their emotional and spiritual needs at the end of life. Hospice care prioritizes comfort and quality of life by reducing pain and suffering. Hospice care provides an alternative to therapies focused on life-prolonging measures that may be arduous, likely to cause more symptoms, or are not aligned with a person's goals.

Informal caregivers — unpaid individuals (for example, a spouse, partner, family member, friend, or neighbor) involved in assisting others with activities of daily living and/or medical tasks.

Joy Camp — These are people within our Key Relationships who bring us joy and provide valuable social connections but are not committed to meet our emotional and practical needs like our Family of Choice. They may journey, over time, closer to or farther from the center.

Key Relationships — These are the people in our Core Relationships who are farther out in our Circles of Connection than our Family of Choice. They are vital, but have fewer expectations and may not be as long term.

Life Compass — Person, People, Place — Being able to know the Person you want to be and how you want to live, who your People and the relationships you want to have with them, and the Place that will help you be at home where your Life Story and contributions are valued and expressed.

Life expectancy — An estimate of the average age that members of a particular population group will be when they die.

Life Planning — A proposal for doing or achieving what is needed to live the life you want based on your values and priorities.

Lifespan — How long you actually live, which could be more or less than life expectancy, because of lifestyle and other factors.

Life Stages — Chronological sections of adult life that each have unique motivations and definitions of success. The list in this book is intended to simply inform our Essential Conversations and Life Compass Planning.

Life Quake — When a life transition happens without warning and/or without a plan, thus making them more traumatic, chaotic, and expensive.

Mindfulness — I use the word to refer to the time and practices a person uses to work on their own self-awareness, personal responsibility, the definition of themselves, and how they show up in relationships. I did not want to use a word that references religious practices, since many people do this work without participation in a faith tradition.

Need — Something that must be provided or accomplished to have the life you want now or in the future.

Outer Connections — These are our social, secondary, and tertiary relationships outside our Core Relationships, which are crucial in order to meet needs and flourish. They are more transactional in nature and usually serve to supply and express the Life Compass Plans rather than define and direct them.

Pathfinders — Individuals in a Family of Choice who are leading, facilitating, and encouraging Essential Conversations and Life Compass Living. There is no guarantee that everyone will follow, but Pathfinders continue Parallel Planning and inviting others to participate.

Parallel Planning — Making plans for our own lives while we walk alongside others who can't or won't make plans with us or as we wish them to.

Pipe Dream — An unattainable or fanciful hope or scheme; hopes without a plan.

Protocols — Structured processes and guidelines to promote meaningful, efficient communication, problem-solving, and learning. Protocols give time for active listening and reflection, and ensure that all voices in the group are heard and honored. Using protocols appropriately in meetings with others helps you build the skills and culture necessary for productive collaborative work.

Resource (noun) — Anyone or anything that meets a current or future need.

Resource (verb) — Dedicating resources to meet a current or future need.

Sandwich generation — A generation of people, typically in their thirties or forties, responsible for bringing up their own children and for the care of their aging parents.

Shared Life Vision — This is the explicit understanding of what is wanted in a relationship as well as how it would look and operate when realized. It will need enough definition to enable those in relationship to define their roles and take responsibility for actualizing that vision.

Stage Characters — Versions of ourselves that serve our anxieties or the expectations of others. They may get us something we want but do not express fidelity to our true or best selves.

Thought Partners — These are the people (friends and professionals) who help us process life at the deeper emotional, spiritual, and mindful levels, where we are deciding who we are and how we want to be in the world. They challenge our views and the decisions we make on our life path, even our Life Compass Plans. They're usually the people that are able to view us through a non-judgmental lens and are more able to nurture us and help us gain needed insights. We feel a sense of energy and encouragement when we're with them.

Trajectory of Readiness — Awareness, Acceptance, and Action — Building our capacity to accept ourselves, others, and life as they are in order to be present and more fully participate in shaping the life we want.

Bibliography

Achor, Shawn, *The Happiness Advantage: How a Positive Brain Fuels Success in Work and Life*. Currency-Crown Publishing Group, 2010

Allen, David, *Getting Things Done: The Art of Stress-free Productivity* (Revised Edition). (Kindle Edition) Penguin Books, 2015

Armstrong, Thomas, *The Human Odyssey: Navigating the 12 Stages of Life*. Sterling Publishing Co. Inc., 2007

Astor, Bart, *Roadmap for the Rest of Your Life: Smart Choices About Money, Health, Work, Lifestyle And Pursuing Your Dreams*. John Wiley & Sons Inc., 2013

Baumeister, Roy F., and Tierney, John, *Willpower: Rediscovering the Greatest Human Strength*. Penguin Books, 2011

Blanchard, Janice M., editor, *Aging in Community (Revised Edition)*. CreateSpace, Second Journey Inc., 2013

Block, Peter, *Community: The Structure of Belonging*. Berrett-Koehler Publishers, 2009

Bowman, Katy, *Dynamic Aging: Simple Exercises for Whole-Body Mobility.* Propriometrics Press, 2017

Bowman, Katy, *Move Your DNA: Restore Your Health Through Natural Movement* (Expanded Edition). Propriometrics Press, 2017

Bradberry, Travis, and Greaves, Jean, *Emotional Intelligence 2.0.* TalentSmart, 2009

Brown, Brene, *Braving the Wilderness: The Quest for True Belonging and the Courage to Stand Alone.* New York, Random House, 2017

Brown, Brene, *The Gifts of Imperfection: Let Go of Who You Think You're Supposed to Be and Embrace Who You Are.* Hazelden Publishing 2010

Brown, Donald E., *Human Universals.* McGraw-Hill Inc., 1991

Brown, Samuel Morris, *Through The Valley of Shadows: Living Wills, Intensive Care, and Making Medicine Human.* Oxford University Press, 2016

Buettner, Dan, *Thrive: Finding Happiness The Blue Zones Way.* National Geographic, 2010

Burnett, Josh, and Hardesey, Pete, *Adulting 101: #WisdomforLife.* BroadStreet Publishing Group LLC, 2018

Burrows, Donald M., *Plan While You Still Can: 16 End-of-life Checklists You Need Now.* Aviva Publishing, 2007

Bush, Karen M., Machinist, Louise S., and Jean McQuillin, *My House, Our House: Living Far Better for Far Less in a Cooperative Household.* St. Lynn's Press, 2013

Cacioppo, John T., and Patrick, William, *Loneliness: Human Nature and the Need for Social Connection.* W.W. Norton & Co. Inc., 2008

Carter, Jimmy, *The Virtues of Aging*. Ballantine Publishing Group, 1998

Carter, Rita, *The Human Brain Book*, 2nd edition. DK Publishing, 2014

Chittister, Joan, *The Gift of Years: Growing Older Gracefully*. New York, Blue Bridge-United Tribes Media Inc., 2008

Christakis, Nicholas A., and Fowler, James H., *Connected: The Surprising Power of Our Social Networks and How They Shape Our Lives*. New York, Little, Brown Spark, 2009

Clear, James, *Atomic Habits: An Easy and Proven Way to Build Good Habits & Break Bad Ones*. Avery, an Imprint of Penguin Random House LLC, 2018

Compernolle, Theo, *Brain Chains: Discover Your Brain and Unleash Its Full Potential in a Hyperconnected Multitasking World*. Compublications, 2014

Covey, Steven R., *Seven Habits of Highly Effective People: Powerful Lessons in Personal Change*. Fireside, a registered trademark of Simon & Schuster, 1989

D'Aprix, Amy S., *From Surviving to Thriving: Transforming Your Caregiving Journey*, Second Life Press, 2008

De Saint-Exupéry, Antoine, *The Little Prince*. Harcourt Inc., 1943, 1971

Dweck, Carol S., *Mindset: How We Can Learn to Fulfill Our Potential*. Random House Publishing Group, 2006

Erikson, Erik H., and Erikson, Joan M., *The Life Cycle Completed* (Extended Edition). W.W. Norton & Co. Inc., 2015

Fisher, Roger, and Ury, William, *Getting to Yes: Negotiating Agreement Without Giving In* (2nd Edition). Penguin Books, 1991

Friedman, Edwin H., *A Failure of Nerve: Leadership in the Age of the Quick Fix*. Seabury Books, 2007

Gawande, Atul, *Being Mortal: Medicine and What Matters in the End*. Metropolitan Books, 2014

Gilbert, Roberta M., *Extraordinary Relationships: A New Way of Thinking About Human Interactions*. John Wiley & Sons Inc., 1992 (Kindle Edition) Leading Systems Press LLC, 2011

Goldsmith, Theodore C., *An Introduction to Biological Aging Theory* (Revised Edition). Crownsville, Maryland, Azinet Press, 2012

Gross, Jane, *A Bittersweet Season: Caring for Our Aging Parents and Ourselves*. Vintage Books-Knopf, 2011

Halifax, Joan, *Being with Dying: Cultivating Compassion and Fearlessness in the Presence of Death*. Shambhala Publications Inc., 2008

Hendrix, Harville, *Getting the Love You Want: A Guide for Couples*. Henry Holt & Co., 1998

Harris, Russ, *The Happiness Trap: How to Stop Struggling and Start Living, A Guide to ACT*. (Kindle Edition) Trumpeter Books, 2011.

Heath, Chip, and Heath, Dan, *The Power of Moments: Why Certain Experiences Have Extraordinary Impact*. Simon & Schuster, 2017

Herring, Hayim, *Connecting Generations: Bridging the Boomer, Gen-X, snd Millennial Divide*. Rowman & Littlefield Publishers, 2019

Hogan, Paul, and Hogan, Lori, *Stages of Senior Care*. McGraw Hill Books, 2010

Huffington, Arianna, *Thrive: The Third Metric to Redefining Success and Creating a Life of Well-Being, Wisdom, and Wonder*. Harmony Books, 2015

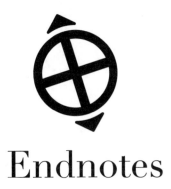

Endnotes

1 | *Loneliness: Human Nature and the Need for Social Connection* by John T. Cacioppo and William Patrick; *Lost Connections: Why You're Depressed and How to Find Hope* by Johann Hari; *The Village Effect: How Face-to-Face Contact Can Make Us Healthier and Happier* by Susan Pinker

2 | *Lost Connections: Why You're Depressed and How to Find Hope* by Johann Hari, page 90

3 | Source: https://charterforcompassion.org/charter

4 | *The Art and Science of Personality Development,* by Dan P. McAdams, Guilford Publications, ©2015, Kindle Edition, page 302.

5 | *The War of Art: Break Through the Blocks and Win Your Inner Creative Battles,* by Steven Pressfield, Black Irish Entertainment ©2002, page 165

6 | *The Happiness Advantage: How a Positive Brain Fuels Success in Work and Life*, by Shawn Achor, Crown Publishing Group ©2010, page 40

7 | Hope for Today, Al-Anon Family Group Headquarters ©2002, page 97

8 | *Emotional Intelligence 2.0*, by Travis Bradberry and Jean Greaves, TalentSmart ©2009

9 | *The Top Five Regrets of the Dying: A Life Transformed by the Dearly Departing*, by Bronnie Ware, ©Bronnie Ware ©2012

10 | *Die Wise: A Manifesto for Sanity and Soul*, by Stephen Jenkinson, North Atlantic Books, ©2015

Patterson, Kerry, et al, *Crucial Conversations: Tools for Talking When Stakes Are High*. McGraw Hill, 2002

Pinker, Susan, *The Village Effect: How Face-To-Face Contact Can Make Us Healthier and Happier*. Spiegel & Grau-Penguin Random House, 2014

Piver, Susan, *The Hard Questions for Adult Children and Their Aging Parents: Facing the Future Together with Courage and Compassion*. Gotham Books, 2004

Pressfield, Steven, *The War of Art: Break Through the Blocks and Win Your Inner Creative Battles*. Black Irish Entertainment LLC, 2002

Rosenberg, Marshall B., *Nonviolent Communication: A Language of Life* (3rd Edition). A PuddleDancer Press Book, 2015

Sheehy, Gail, *Passages in Caregiving: Turning Chaos Into Confidence*. William Morrow-HarperCollins Books, 2011

Sinek, Simon, *Start With Why: How Great Leaders Inspire Everyone to Take Action*. London, Penguin Books, 2009

Solie, David, *How to Say It to Seniors: Closing the Communication Gap with Our Elders*. Prentiss Hall Press, 2004

Solomon, Sheldon, Greenberg, Jeff, and Pyszezynski, Tom, *The Worm at the Core: On the Role of Death in Life*. New York, Penguin Random House, 2015

Thomas, Bill, *Second Wind: Navigating the Passage to a Slower, Deeper and More Connected Life*. (Kindle Edition) New York, Simon & Schuster, 2014

Thomas, William H., *What Are Old People For? How Elders Will Save The World*. VanderWyk & Burnham, 2007

Vaillant, George E., *Aging Well: Surprising Guideposts to a Happier Life from the Landmark Harvard Study of Adult Development* (First Ebook Edition). New York, Little, Brown Spark-Hatchette Book Group, 2002

Van der Kolk, Bessel, *The Body Keeps the Score: Brain, Mind, and Body in the Healing of Trauma*. New York, Viking-Penguin Books, 2014

Volandes, Angelo E., *The Conversation: A Revolutionary Plan for End-of-Life Care*. New York, Bloomsbury, 2015

Ware, Bronnie, *The Top Five Regrets of the Dying: A Life Transformed by the Dearly Departing*. Balboa Press-Hay House, 2012

Hyatt, Michael, and Harkavy, Daniel, *Living Forward: A Proven Plan to Stop Drifting and Get the Life You Want.* Baker Books, 2016

Irving, Paul H., *The Upside of Aging: How Long Life Is Changing the World of Health, Work, Innovation, Policy, and Purpose.* John Wiley & Sons Inc., 2014

Jenkinson, Stephen, *Come of Age: The Case for Elderhood in a Time of Trouble.* North Atlantic Books, 2018

Jenkinson, Stephen, *Die Wise: A Manifesto for Sanity and Soul.* North Atlantic Books, 2015

Kalanithi, Paul, *When Breath Becomes Air.* Random House, 2016

Kelaher, Hope, *Here to Make Friends: How to Make Friends As An Adult.* Ulysses Press, 2020

Kind, Viki, *The Caregiver's Path to Compassionate Decision-making: Making Choices for Those Who Can't.* Greenleaf Book Group, 2010

Kurtz, Ernest, and Ketcham, Katherine, *The Spirituality of Imperfection: Storytelling and the Journey to Wholeness.* Bantam, 1992

Landry, Roger, *Live Long, Die Short: A Guide to Authentic Health and Successful Aging.* Greenleaf Book Group Press, 2014

Leider, Richard J., and Shapiro, David A., *Claiming Your Place at the Fire: Living the Second Half of Your Life on Purpose.* San Francisco. Berrett-Koehler Publishers Inc., 2004

Leider, Richard J., and Webber, Alan M., *Life Reimagined: Discovering Your New Life Possibilities.* Berrett-Koehler Publishers Inc. 2013

The Life Planning Network, *Live Smart after 50! The Experts' Guide to Life Planning for Uncertain Times.* Boston, Life Planning Network Inc., 2012

May, Gerald G., *Addiction and Grace.* Harper & Row Publishers, 1988

McAdams, Dan P., *The Art and Science of Personality Development*. The Guilford Press, 2015

McAdams, Dan P. *The Stories We Live By: Personal Myths and the Making of the Self*. William Morrow and Co. Inc., 1993

Miller, William R. and Rollnick Stephen, *Motivational interviewing: Helping People Change* (3rd Edition). The Guilford Press, 2013

Moody, Harry R., and Sasser, Jennifer R., *Aging: Concepts and Controversies*. Sage Publications, 2015

Moore, Thomas, *Ageless Soul: The Lifelong Journey Toward Meaning and Joy*. St. Martin's Press, 2017

Morris, Virginia, *How to Care for Aging Parents*. Workman Publishing Co., 2004

Myers, Joseph R., *The Search to Belong: Rethinking Intimacy, Community and Small Groups*. Zondervan, 2003

Ornish, Dean, *Love and Survival: 8 Pathways to Intimacy and Health*. William Morrow-HarperCollins, 1999

Ornish, Dean, and Ornish, Anne, *Undo It! How Simple Lifestyle Changes Can Reverse Most Chronic Diseases*. Ballantine Books-Penguin Random House, 2019

Orsi, Janelle, and Doskow, Emily, *The Sharing Solution: How to Save Money, Simplify Your Life and Build Community*. Nolo, 2009

Palmer, Parker J., *On the Brink of Everything: Grace, Gravity & Getting Old*. Berrett-Koehler Publishers Inc., 2018

Parker, Prya, *The Art of Gathering: How We Meet and Why It Matters*. Riverhead Books-Penguin Random House, 2018